THE
SPIRIT
AND
SERVICE
IN
SPIRIT

WITNESS LEE

Living Stream Ministry
Anaheim, California

First Edition, January 2001.

ISBN 0-7363-1159-9

Published by

Living Stream Ministry
2431 W. La Palma Ave., Anaheim, CA 92801 U.S.A.
P. O. Box 2121, Anaheim, CA 92814 U.S.A.

Printed in the United States of America

01 02 03 04 05 06 07 / 9 8 7 6 5 4 3 2 1

CONTENTS

Title   *Page*

Preface   5

1 The Fundamental Matter of Service   7

2 Our Spirit Having Been Deadened and Made Alive   21

3 Only Our Spirit Being Able to Contact God   39

4 The Sense of the Spirit and Knowing the Spirit   55

5 Discerning the Soul from the Spirit   67

6 The Service Which Is in Spirit   81

7 The Rejecting and Tearing Down of the Soul   93

8 The Service Which Is from God   105

PREFACE

This book is a translation of messages given in Chinese by Brother Witness Lee. They were first published in *The Ministry of the Word* in 1951 through 1954. These messages were not reviewed by the speaker.

CHAPTER ONE

THE FUNDAMENTAL MATTER OF SERVICE

Scripture Reading: John 4:21, 23-24

In these messages we will consider the matter of the spirit and the service in the spirit. We will see what the spirit is and what the service in the spirit is. In other words, we will consider what our service should be before God and with what and in what we should serve.

If we want to know how we should serve before God, we need to be clear about the fundamental matter of service. In John 4 the Lord Jesus referred to the fundamental matter of worship. The worship to which the Lord Jesus referred, in a narrow sense, means to bow down to God. In a broader sense, it means to serve God, including all the positive matters between God and us, such as our drawing near to God, praying to God, looking unto God, waiting on God, having fellowship with God, and working for God. Therefore, the fundamental matter of worship spoken of by the Lord Jesus is also the fundamental matter of service. Concerning this matter, the Lord Jesus mentioned two basic points.

GOD BEING SPIRIT

Our service and worship have an object. We do not serve emptiness, nor do we worship nothingness. We serve and worship because we have a real object. The object of our service and worship is not a thing or a common person, nor is it a matter or a work; rather, it is God. God is the object of our service and worship. If there were no God, then we would have no worship or service, and we would have no need of worship or service. We have worship and service because there is God and because God needs our worship and service.

All our service and worship are toward God. The One whom we serve and worship is God. When we mention worship and service, we should think of God and God only. This is because God, and only God, is the object of our service and worship.

If we want our service to be proper, then we need to have a proper knowledge of the object of our service. The object of our service is none other than God. God is Spirit. God is nothing other than Spirit. God is neither a material thing nor a psychological object; He is neither a doctrine nor a concept; He is neither a theory nor an "ism." He is Spirit. God is not a material thing that can be touched by our hands or seen by our eyes. Neither is God a psychological object that can be imagined by our mind or contacted by our intellect. Rather, God is Spirit. As such, He cannot be sensed by any part of our body or be contacted by any part of our soul. Spirit is neither material nor psychological, but transcends the material and the psychological.

In contacting something, one must know what it is and what its nature is before one can have proper contact. For instance, if you know something is a sound, you contact it with your ears. If it is a color, you contact it with your eyes. If it is a smell, you contact it with your nose. If it is a concept or theory, you contact it with your mind. When you contact these various items based on your understanding of them, your contact is proper; otherwise, it is wrong.

Whenever we contact God and serve God, we must know and understand what kind of God He is and what His nature is. Then our contact with God and our service to Him will be proper and not absurd. We must know and realize that God is not a material thing or a psychological object. Rather, God is Spirit. We must also remember that since God is Spirit, He cannot be felt with our body, nor can He be contacted with our soul. In this way our service toward God will be proper.

SERVING GOD IN SPIRIT

The Lord Jesus said, "God is Spirit, and those who worship Him must worship in spirit" (John 4:24). Since God is *Spirit,* we who worship Him must worship with our *spirit* and in our *spirit;* otherwise, our worship is improper and absurd. Our worship and service to God must be in spirit. Whatever positive relationships we have with God must all be in our spirit and not in our body or in our mind. The Lord Jesus said, "The true worshippers will worship the Father in spirit" (v. 23). Only those who worship and serve in spirit are *true* worshippers. If you merely prostrate yourself before God, or if you merely pray, praise, or invent a kind of service to God with your mind, these things do not constitute a true worship or service. They might be considered a kind of worship or service, but they do not constitute the *true* worship and the *true* service. True worship and true service are in spirit.

The Lord Jesus also said, "Neither in this mountain nor in Jerusalem will you worship the Father" (v. 21). This tells us that worship or service to God does not depend on the place. Even if you kneel in obeisance in a cathedral, this might still not be the true worship. True worship does not depend on the place or the building. It does not depend on anything physical or outward. Rather, it depends on the spirit. Only the worship, the service, that is in spirit is true. Regardless of how much piety, reverence, worship, or service there is, if it is not in spirit, it is not true and does not have much value in the eyes of God.

God is seeking after the worship and service that are in spirit. Because He is Spirit, if we want to worship and serve Him, we must do so by using our spirit. You cannot use your hands to touch or your mind to think about anything that is spirit. God is Spirit; therefore, you cannot contact Him with outward things, with material things, with your body, or with your mind. Since He is Spirit, you must contact Him with your spirit. If you try to contact Him with anything that is not spirit, it does not work. Only the spirit can contact and touch the Spirit. He is Spirit, but if you do not contact Him with your spirit, you cannot touch Him, even though He is real.

I often say that if you want to touch electricity, you must use a conductor. Metals are conductors. When you touch an electrical source with metal, electricity is transmitted. But if you touch an electrical source with a wooden stick, no electricity will be transmitted because you are using the wrong thing.

God is Spirit. Therefore, if you want to contact Him, worship Him, or serve Him, you need to use your spirit. If you use anything other than your spirit to contact Him, worship Him, or serve Him, then on the one hand, He will not be able to receive true worship and service, and on the other hand, you will not be able to receive true inspiration. Although many people often worship God, they are not moved or inspired inwardly because they do not contact God with their spirit. Consider electric fans; they keep turning because they are in contact with electricity. Once they come in contact with electricity, they begin to rotate. Whenever our spirit contacts and touches God, we are inwardly moved and inspired. If one prays to God and worships God, yet he is not inwardly moved, this does not mean that there is no God or that there is a problem with God. Rather, it means there is something wrong with the praying and worshipping one. Perhaps instead of using his spirit, he tries to use his mind or his bodily senses to contact God. Actually, neither his mind nor his body can enable him to come into contact with God or to receive inner inspiration from God.

We all know that if we insert a small piece of paper or wood in an electrical outlet, the electric fan immediately stops turning. Although the fan might be very close to the electricity, it cannot make contact with the electricity. Likewise, today many people are close to God. They acknowledge the existence of God and have the fear of God in their hearts. They often read the Bible, listen to sermons, and go to church to worship God. But they have not touched God, nor have they been moved by God. This is because they do not use their spirit to contact God. Although they are near God, there is still a problem between them and God. They use things other than the spirit to contact God. They may be sitting or kneeling properly with their body, thinking about God in their mind, and inclining toward God in their heart, yet they are not able to touch God. This is because man cannot contact God in his body, in his mind, or even in his heart. God is

Spirit. Man must be in spirit in order to contact, worship, or serve God. Only by being in the spirit can man meet God and touch God.

MAN HAVING A SPIRIT

We have said many times that both the Scriptures and our experiences tell us that man is of three parts: spirit, soul, and body. Man not only has a body and a soul, but he also has a spirit (1 Thes. 5:23). Just as the body and the soul are separate, so the spirit and the soul are also divided (Heb. 4:12). The body, which has a form, is the outward, visible part of man, including the limbs and the various parts of human anatomy. The soul, which is without a form, is the inner, invisible part of man as his personality, his real self; it includes the human mind, will, and emotion. Man's thoughts, intentions, preferences, and feelings of happiness, anger, sadness, or joy are all functions of the human soul. The spirit, which is also without a form, is the innermost part of man; it includes man's conscience, the intuition of God, and fellowship with God. Man contacts the physical things through the body, the psychological things through the soul, and the things of God through the spirit.

Therefore, outwardly man has a body that belongs to the physical realm, and inwardly he has a soul that belongs to the psychological realm. Furthermore, in his innermost being he has a spirit, which is neither physical nor psychological. This spirit is the highest thing of the created life. Man is higher than all the other created things on the earth because man has a spirit, which none of the others have. Not to mention the lifeless things, even the living creatures other than man do not have a spirit.

Plants have life, but they do not have a spirit or even a soul; they are without the mind, emotion, or will. The plant life, the lowest life, is without consciousness.

Although the animal life is higher than the plant life, it also does not have a spirit. The animal life is higher than the plant life because animals have a soul. Animals such as puppies, kittens, little monkeys, and small birds possess a life that is higher than the plant life because they have a soul with a mind, emotion, and will. A puppy or a kitten has a mind, emotion, and will. They can decide to do or not to do a certain thing. If you treat them well, they will feel at ease and they will like you. If you mistreat them, they will feel miserable and they will dislike you. This is because within them there is the function of the soul. Despite the fact that they have a soul, they still do not have a spirit.

Among all the creatures on the earth, only man has a spirit. Therefore, man is higher than all the other creatures, including both plants and animals. Within man there is not only the soul, including the mind, the emotion, and the will, but there is another thing, which is higher than and superior to the soul. This higher life which is within man is the spirit of man. Although this life of the spirit of man is lower than the uncreated life of God, it is higher than all the other created lives.

Man is higher than all the other creatures not only because man's mind is intelligent, his will is strong, and his emotion is rich; even the more it is because there is a spirit in man. The most important reason that man is higher than and different from all the other creatures is that man has a spirit within, while the other creatures do not.

GOD'S INTENTION IN CREATING MAN WITH A SPIRIT

God put a spirit in man, that is, He created man with a spirit, because He wanted man to worship and serve Him. He created man for Himself. He wanted man to have a relationship with Him by worshipping and serving Him. Since He is Spirit and since He wanted to create a man who would worship and serve Him, then how could man worship and serve God unless He created man with a spirit? For instance, there is air outside of man, but if man does not have a breathing organ, how can he contact air and take it in? Even though he is in contact with the air outwardly, he still does not have a relationship with the air inwardly. To have an inward relationship with the air he must have a breathing organ to receive the air into him. Likewise, man must have a spirit to contact God, who is Spirit.

God is Spirit, and He created man that man might worship and serve Him as Spirit. Therefore, He created man with a spirit to enable man to contact Him as Spirit and to worship and serve Him as Spirit. To further illustrate, there is sound in the universe and God wants man to hear it, so He created man with ears. If God had not created man with ears, man would not be able to hear, even though sound exists in the universe and God also wants man to hear it. Likewise, if God did not create man with a spirit, man would have no way to contact Him as Spirit, even though He as Spirit exists in the universe and He also wants man to contact Him as Spirit. Since God desired that man contact Him, worship Him, and serve Him as Spirit, He needed to create man with a spirit, which He did.

God created man with a spirit because His intention is that man should worship and serve Him. Although some animals, such as monkeys, dogs, cats, and parrots, are very intelligent and clever, none of them has a desire to worship God. No one has ever seen a dog or a cat worshipping God. Neither has anyone seen a monkey building a little temple to worship God. Animals do not worship God, nor do they desire to worship God, because they do not have a spirit. Man, however, is different. People in the world, whether they have culture or they have no culture, whether they are civilized or they are barbaric, whether they are wise or they are foolish, all have a thought and a desire to worship God. When you travel throughout the world, you cannot find a people that do not have the worship of God. The way they worship may be wrong and the object of their worship may be wrong and false, but the desire within them to worship God is still proper and genuine. Without exception among the human race, all people in the world have the inner thought and desire to worship God. This is because within every human being there is a God-created spirit for him to worship God.

THE NEED OF THE SPIRIT

Man has a spirit, so he has the need of the spirit. What the spirit needs is God. The spirit was created for man to contact God, so it needs God. This is just like the stomach, which needs food because it was created for man to receive food. If there were no food, there would be no need to have a stomach; if there were no stomach, there would also be no need to have food. Likewise, if there were no God, there would be no need for the human spirit, and if there were no human spirit, man would also have no need for God. However, man has a spirit, and man's spirit came into existence for man to contact God; therefore, man needs God.

Man has various kinds of needs. Because man has three parts—body, soul, and spirit—he has three different kinds of needs. Man has a body, so he has the needs of the body. Man has a soul, so he has the needs of the soul. Likewise, man has a spirit, so he has the needs of the spirit. The needs of the body are physical, the needs of the soul are psychological, and the needs of the spirit are spiritual. Man has at least these three kinds of needs: physical needs, psychological needs, and spiritual needs. Only when these three kinds of needs are met can man feel no lack or emptiness.

The physical needs—the needs for clothing, food, housing, and transportation—are all for man's body. The human body needs clothes for covering, food for eating, houses for dwelling, and the means of transportation for traveling. These are all material needs. Today people pay attention mostly to these material needs. They are very concerned about the matters of clothing, food, housing, and transportation, which are all related to the body. This is especially true with the poor. A poor man eats badly, clothes himself poorly, has a problem with housing, and has difficulty in transportation. Therefore, all he thinks about from morning to evening are these material needs. Besides these, it seems that he does not feel he has other needs. It seems that in his feeling these material things are all his needs.

Then one day he may make a fortune and have a large amount of money. Then he is well-fed and well-dressed, he lives in a mansion, and he rides in a car. But when all the problems of food, clothing, housing, and transportation are solved, when all the material needs are satisfied, he will discover that besides the material needs there is another kind of need, the psychological needs. He will discover that once the problem of material needs is taken care of, then the problem of psychological needs comes. Previously he felt that his body needed food, clothes, a house, and a car; besides these needs, it seemed that he did not feel the need for anything else. But now he feels that, in addition to the needs of his body, he needs pleasure and enjoyment psychologically. He now wants to watch movies, listen to music, and read novels and newspapers. He also likes to travel and seek recreation and entertainment. Now he does not feel his physical needs very much; rather, he strongly feels his psychological needs. These psychological needs are for the satisfaction of the human soul and not of the human body.

Man does not only have these two kinds of needs, the needs of the body and the needs of the soul. When man has satisfied his physical needs and psychological needs, he discovers that there is still a need in his deepest part, his innermost part. Before man satisfies his outward, material needs, he does not have much sense of his psychological needs. Likewise, before man solves his inward, psychological needs, he does not feel so much the need in his deepest being. After a man satisfies his outward, material needs and takes care of his inward, psychological needs, the innermost need in his being will surface and will be felt by him. When the outward, material needs and the inward, psychological needs of man are satisfied and solved, man senses that there is still a need in his deepest part. Moreover, the richer his material enjoyment is and the more satisfying his psychological entertainment is, the more he senses the need in his innermost being. Although he does not know what this need is, he can sense it. He cannot explain it, but he can sense its existence. This need, which is a spiritual need, is not for man's body or for his soul but for his spirit. Because man has a body, he has material needs. Because man has a soul, he has psychological needs. In the same way, because man has a spirit, he has a spiritual need. This spiritual need cannot be satisfied by material things or by psychological things; this spiritual need can be satisfied only by God.

The human spirit was created neither for material enjoyment nor for psychological pleasure. Therefore, neither material enjoyment nor psychological pleasure can satisfy or meet the need in the human spirit. The human spirit was created for God. Hence, only God can satisfy the human spirit and meet its need. What the human spirit needs is God. The spirit of man needs God, thirsts for God, and seeks after God. Man's need for God is a matter of the need in the spirit; it is not a matter of the intellect in the human mind. The need for God in the deepest part of man, which is his spirit, will not disappear just because his mind cannot understand it, nor will it diminish just by his reasoning in the mind. This is a matter of need, not a matter of reason. Within man there is a spirit, which has a spiritual need. The need of the human spirit is for God.

Someone may be successful and famous and may have a very good family. His material enjoyments are rich, and his psychological pleasures are complete. In others' eyes it seems that he is fully blessed and has no lack in anything and should therefore be very satisfied. But he himself still feels there is a need and therefore pursues God with such a hunger and thirst. To others, it seems that such a lucky person as he is should simply be at peace and enjoy life. Thus, they wonder why he should be pursuing God, why he should be engaging himself in such an unnecessary endeavor, and why he should be so superstitious. But in his feeling all these things are necessary; they satisfy the need in his deepest being. In his feeling this need is more important than the outward needs of his body for material enjoyment and deeper than the inward needs of his soul for psychological pleasures. This feeling is so intense that, if necessary for his pursuit of God and for the gaining of what he needs in his deepest part, he is willing even to sacrifice material enjoyments and psychological pleasures. The reason he pursues God by sacrificing everything and not caring for anything else is that there is this need in his deepest part, in his spirit.

Every organ and faculty of the human body has its need and the object of its need. The ears need sound, the eyes need colors, the mouth needs tasty things, the nose needs air, and the stomach needs food and water. Because man has these organs and faculties, he has these needs and the objects of these needs. Likewise, man has a spirit, and the spirit of man has its need and the object of its need also. This object is God. God is what the spirit of man needs. It is not enough for man to just care for the needs of his ears, eyes, mouth, nose, and stomach; man must also satisfy the need of his spirit. The need of man's spirit cannot be satisfied by material things. Only God can satisfy the need of man's spirit because man's spirit was created for God.

If the various faculties and organs of the human body cannot obtain what they need, they will be miserable. If you were put in confinement so that your ears could not hear any sound and your eyes could not see any scenery, you would feel that to be unbearable. Even the more, if your nose could not breathe in the air and your stomach could not take in food or water, you would feel more miserable. You would give up the whole world just to be able to breathe in the air; you would rather have food and water than bars of gold. In the same way, when the spirit of man cannot obtain what it needs, it feels very uneasy. For this reason, a man often would rather give up the world and sacrifice everything in order to pursue after God and gain Him.

God wants man to worship and serve Him, so He created man with a spirit. The spirit in man causes man to sense the need for God and thus to thirst for God and pursue after God. This is something that transcends human reason and is not up to man himself. We were created by God. God wants us to worship and serve Him; therefore, He prepared a faculty for us to worship and serve Him, which is the spirit within us. This spirit causes us to feel the need to worship and serve God. If we agree in our intellect to worship and serve God, our spirit causes us to sense this need. Even if we do not agree, our spirit still causes us to sense this need. This is similar to the way our stomach causes us to sense the need to eat. It does not matter if our intellect agrees or disagrees; the stomach causes us to feel such a need. This feeling is outside of and beyond our intellect.

Brothers and sisters, please remember that there is a spirit in man, that there is a need in the spirit of man, and that this need is for God. Not to mention the believers, even the unbelievers also need God in their spirit. They feel that they need something inside. Although they do not realize that this something is God, they feel that there is this need. As saved ones, we have an even greater sense of this need. This morning if you did not draw near to God, pray to Him, open up yourself to Him to fellowship with Him, or breathe God in with your spirit, then surely you are unhappy and feel that there is a lack within you. But if you prayed to God, worshipped Him, and contacted Him this morning, you feel inwardly refreshed and satisfied. This is because there is a spirit in you, and the need of the spirit is for God.

THE FEELING OF THE SPIRIT

The spirit within man not only has its need but also has its feeling. The body has its physical feelings. When a person is cut by a knife or beaten with a rod, he feels pain outwardly; this is the feeling of the body. When someone is ridiculed or rebuked, he feels pain inwardly. This is not a physical feeling but a psychological feeling, a feeling of the soul. Beside these two kinds of feelings, the physical feeling and the psychological feeling, there is another kind of feeling which is in the deepest part of man. Sometimes we feel pain and sorrow in our deepest part. That feeling of pain is not physical or psychological. It is deeper than the psychological feeling; it is the feeling of the spirit.

Many times you want to do a certain thing. Your mind thinks it is reasonable, and your relatives and friends all approve of it and consider it sensible, but there is something in your deepest part, your innermost part, that disagrees with it and says it is wrong. There is a feeling in your deepest part; this feeling is the feeling in your spirit, which transcends the physical feeling and the psychological feeling. It transcends the mind and intellect, and it transcends the soul. The feeling of the spirit is not psychological or mental, and even the more it is not physical. Rather, it is a feeling in the deepest part of man. In particular, when one does something immoral or something shameful, in his depths he feels unsettled or uneasy. His intellect, his mind, his consideration, and his thought may let him go, but this feeling in his deepest part does not let him go. Regardless of how his intellect agrees with it and how his thought justifies it, the feeling of his spirit deep within him neither approves or justifies it.

The spirit was created by God for man to contact Him; hence, the feeling of the spirit is especially keen with respect to God. The spirit of man causes him not only to sense the need for God but also to sense God Himself. Very often the mind and intellect of man consider the existence of God illogical, yet the spirit of man senses that there is God. Very often the mind and thought of man cannot perceive the things of God, yet the spirit of man can sense the things of God. The sense of the spirit is a direct faculty for man to perceive God. It is through the sense of the spirit that God enables man to know Him and perceive the things that are of Him. Because man has the sense of the spirit and is able to know God and perceive the things of God, man can worship and serve God. Since man can know God and perceive the things of God only through the sense of the spirit, man must worship and serve God through and in the spirit.

THE FUNDAMENTAL MATTER OF SERVICE

Therefore, the fundamental matter of service is a matter of our spirit and the Spirit. God is Spirit, and we have a spirit within us. God as Spirit wants our spirit to serve Him. Therefore, service is a matter of our spirit serving the Spirit, that is, the spirit of man serving, worshipping, contacting, and having fellowship with the Spirit of God. Only this kind of service is the *true* service.

The religions of the world teach people how to worship and serve God. That worship and service, according to the Lord's word, are mostly not true. Even the worship and service in our midst today also may not be completely true, and it is possible, even very likely, that some of them are not true at all. Much of the worship and service that we consider right and good may in fact be wrong and not true in the Lord's eyes because they are not rendered in spirit. Only the worship and service rendered in spirit are the true worship and service.

CHAPTER TWO

OUR SPIRIT HAVING BEEN DEADENED AND MADE ALIVE

Scripture Reading: Eph. 2:1-5; Col. 2:13; John 1:14; 3:3, 6; 6:63; 14:16-20

In the previous message we saw that God wants man to serve Him in spirit and that only the service which is in spirit can enable man to touch Him. Therefore God created man with a spirit by which man may serve Him.

THE FUNCTION OF OUR SPIRIT

The spirit as the innermost part of man is the kernel of man. Man's being man lies in his spirit. Man is not for the existence of the body or for the enjoyment of the soul but for the service of God in spirit.

The function of the spirit within man is to enable man to know God, serve God, contact God, and have fellowship with God. Just as man cannot contact God with the five senses of his body, neither can he touch God with the mind, emotion, and will of his soul. Neither the body nor the soul can get through to God; only the spirit of man can. Man can only contact and touch God in, through, and with his spirit.

OUR SPIRIT HAVING BEEN DEADENED

Because man sinned and became fallen, the spirit in man became dead. When Adam sinned, not only did it cause him to have a record of sin before God and to have the nature of sin within him, but it also caused the spirit in him to become dead. God told him that in the day he ate of the tree of the knowledge of good and evil he would surely die. But after he ate of it, outwardly he did not die. Even though outwardly his body did not die and his outward man was still alive, the spirit within him was deadened and lost its fellowship with God. In other words, it lost its function and feeling. From that time on, due to sin, the spirit in man was deadened to God and had lost its function with respect to God.

The spirit within man is deadened and "deflated"; therefore, it has lost its function and its consciousness. This may be compared to the deadness of the ears of someone who is deaf. A deaf person is not without ears. He has ears, but his ears have lost their function and their sensation; thus, his ears have died. Today although there is a spirit in man, it is dead. Originally the spirit within man enabled him to sense and contact God, but now because the spirit has been deadened, it has lost its function and its sense. Therefore, it cannot sense or contact God, just as the ears of a deaf person are unable to sense or contact sound. To a deaf person, it is as if there were no sound. Likewise, to a person whose spirit is dead, it is as if there were no God.

Today, man's fall not only has caused the spirit of man to lose its sense and function and therefore become dead; it has even caused man not to realize or know that he has a spirit. Man does not know how to use his spirit to contact God, nor is he even aware that he has a spirit. Man only knows that he has a body and a soul with the mind, emotion, and will; he is not aware that he has a spirit. Man realizes that he has a body to contact the physical things and a soul with the mind, emotion, and will to contact the psychological things. He does not realize, however, that he has a spirit to contact the spiritual things, the things of God. Because man does not know that he has a spirit, he basically does not use his spirit to contact God. Thus, he is unable to contact God or sense God. Consequently, he feels and thinks that there is no God. This is similar to a blind person thinking that there are no colors. Although colors exist, he cannot touch them with his hands, smell them with his nose, or hear them with his ears. In his sensation it is as if colors do not exist, because his faculty for perceiving colors has been lost. Likewise, God does exist, but man does not sense God's existence because man is ignorant of the fact that he has a spirit and therefore fails to use the proper faculty, the spirit within him, to contact God.

The spirit of man has lost its feeling and function, and it has become dead to such an extent that even its existence is not felt. This is due to the fact that man has fallen into sin and lives in sin. Therefore, the Bible says, "You, though dead in your offenses and sins" (Eph. 2:1) and "You, though dead in your offenses and in the uncircumcision of your flesh" (Col. 2:13). Sin causes the spirit of man to lose its feeling and function and to become dead. The more one lives in sins, the more his spirit loses its sense and function and becomes more deadened. The more one lives according to his flesh, the more he does not sense that he has a spirit.

THE RISING UP OF THE SOUL AND THE FLESH

Because the spirit of man has lost its sense and function and therefore has become dead, and because man does not sense that he has a spirit, man lives according to the soul and the flesh. The spirit of a fallen man is dead, but his soul and his flesh are still living. Furthermore, because his spirit has been deadened, his soul has gained a greater position. Formerly his spirit was taking the lead within, but now since his spirit is dead, his soul has assumed the leading position. His spirit could be connected with God, could contact God, and could be under God's ruling. But now it is different with his soul. His soul cannot be connected with God but can only be connected with itself. It cannot contact God but can only remain in itself; it does not like to be under God's ruling but likes to act according to its own will. Since his soul has assumed the leading position to rule over him and to control him, which was previously occupied by his spirit, this makes him unable to contact God and causes him to dislike being under God's ruling. Thus, he can only remain in himself and walk according to his own will. Consequently, this gives his flesh the opportunity to indulge in lust. Therefore, a person who is deadened in his spirit is dead in offenses and sins and conducts himself in the lusts of the flesh, doing the desires of the flesh and of the thoughts, which are the result of the operation of the mind in the soul (Eph. 2:3).

The spirit of man is the core and the center of man. Man ought to let the spirit take the lead and walk according to the spirit. Under normal circumstances, man ought to live in the spirit and be controlled by the spirit. After contacting God and receiving His commands, the spirit directs the soul. The soul in turn directs the body, and the body takes action. In this way whatever man does is according to the will of God and is pleasing to Him.

But man fell and man's spirit became deadened. Man's core became "deflated" and man's center lost its function. Now man's soul rises up to replace the spirit. Because the spirit is deadened, the soul rises up. When the soul rises up, it causes man to act according to whatever he likes.

Due to the fall, Satan's life, that is, the satanic nature, entered into man's body. This satanic nature becomes the lust in man's body that causes man to sin, and this lust is referred to in Romans 7 as "the law of sin which is in my members" (v. 23). Since the lust for sinning is present in man's body, man's body becomes the flesh. This flesh of man is very cooperative with man's soul. Since the soul, after rising up to take the place of the spirit, causes man to do according to whatever he likes, the flesh comes to help the soul to do evil. Man's soul represents man's self, while man's flesh represents sin. The union of man's soul with man's flesh is thus a marriage between man and sin. The result is that man does many different things to offend and oppose God. All the evil things done by man are the issue of the union of these two. Since man walks according to these two, the soul and the flesh, instead of allowing the spirit to take the lead and walking according to the spirit, man becomes "soulish" (1 Cor. 2:14) and "fleshly" (3:3).

All the things that the soulish and fleshly man does according to the soul and the flesh are against God and are not pleasing to God, yet they may not appear sinful or bad outwardly. In fact, some of them may seem to be quite good. Nevertheless, they are carried out by the body under the direction of the soul; hence, they are not of the spirit. Therefore, they are also not of God and they are not pleasing to God.

Although the spirit of man has been deadened, his soul and his flesh still have their desires and works, and although these desires and works are not of his spirit, outwardly they are not necessarily bad. Even though they come out of the preferences of his soul and his flesh, some of them are good on the surface.

Some people are cruel by nature and delight in hating others. Thus, their living and their behavior exhibit their hatred for others mostly according to the desire of their inborn nature of hate. But others are kind by nature and readily love people. Thus, their living and their behavior show their love toward others mostly under the direction of the desire of their inborn nature of love. According to these two things—love and hate—loving others is better than hating others; loving others is right and hating others is wrong. But from the spiritual viewpoint, just as hate comes from man's self, love also comes from man's self. One who hates others surely has not touched or contacted God. Likewise, one who loves others may also have not touched or contacted God. In others words, both the one who hates and the one who loves do not hate or love out of their contact with God in their human spirit. Just as the hatred of that one is not the issue of his contact with God in spirit, so the love of this one is also not the issue of his contact with God in spirit. That one's hating others is his behavior; it is not his service to God. Likewise, this one's loving others is his behavior and is not his service to God.

Christians ought to love, but there are at least two kinds of Christian love. One kind of love is of God and is by the spirit; another kind of love is of the Christian himself and is by the soul and the flesh. The former is spiritual; the latter is natural. While the former requires the Christian to contact and touch God, the latter does not. The Christian with the second kind of love was born with a love for others; his natural disposition is to love others. Whomever he meets, he has to show at least some amount of love; otherwise, he does not feel good. If he can show some love and render a little help, then he feels contented and happy. Many Christians have this kind of love. They love not because of their contact and touch with God but because of their natural disposition. They have this kind of love without having to contact or touch God, and even without having to confess the existence of God. Even before they were saved, before they knew God, and before they confessed that there is a God, they already had such a love. They were born with this kind of love. Then after they were saved, they brought this love into the church. The brothers and sisters who do not know the spiritual matters adequately would say that this kind of love is spiritual and that the Christians who love in this way are also spiritual. However, brothers and sisters, if this is being spiritual, then these ones were already spiritual before they were saved. Someone may have been saved for only two years, yet before he was saved, he was already like a sheep and he liked to love others, sympathize with others, and help others. If we say that this is being spiritual, then this person would have become spiritual without the need to be saved and made alive in the spirit. Therefore, this kind of love is not spiritual. Rather, it is what one possesses naturally. One does not need to contact or depend on God in order to have this kind of love. One can have it by birth.

This kind of love and, in the same principle, this kind of goodness and virtue are right, proper, and good, as far as human behavior is concerned. But brothers and sisters, the Lord's salvation is not merely for us to behave well and be an outstanding, respectable person. Rather, it is for us to serve God and to contact God in all things in our daily life that we may live and express Him. Therefore, in the church there is another kind of Christian whose love and virtue come from his contact with God and trust in God. Some of these believers might have been cruel and wicked previously, but now they love God, draw near to God, and contact God with their spirit. God is love, and God is rich in virtues. Therefore, when they contact God and touch God from within, they contact love and touch virtue. They allow God to fill them up in their spirit so that their spirit is strengthened to overcome their soul and their flesh. Therefore, God's love and virtue are lived out through them spontaneously. This kind of love and virtue is not of themselves but of God and yet through them. They are not the source; the source is God. This kind of love and virtue is not only their deeds toward others but also their service to God. Although this is their living, it is even the more their service to God. Because they draw near to God, contact God, and have fellowship with God, they are able to live in their spirit and allow God to pass through them and be manifested in them. This kind of living allows God to obtain their service and worship. Actually, this kind of living is their service and worship to God. Apparently, this is merely their conduct or behavior, but tracing back to the origin, this is their contact with God which allows Him to pass through them and be manifested in them so that He may receive their service and worship.

Some of the brothers and sisters live this way in the spirit so that God may receive their service and worship. However, most Christians do not live like this. The Christians who are defeated and who indulge in their lusts surely do not live like this. However, even many Christians who live cautiously and who are full of love and virtue do not live this way. Their love and virtue are what they naturally delight in. They can live out love and virtue by themselves without contacting God or allowing God to pass through them. Therefore, this love and virtue, which are natural and not spiritual, are the good living that comes out of the Christians themselves, not the spiritual service that comes out of God.

Therefore, a person who is deadened in spirit does not and cannot live by the spirit. Rather, he lives by the soul and according to the flesh. Nevertheless, all that he lives out and all that he does may not appear to be bad. In fact, some of it may even appear to be quite good. However, even though it is good, it is not by or of the spirit. Instead, it is by the soul and according to the flesh. No matter what is being expressed in his outward living, inwardly he is always living by and according to the soul and the flesh.

Man is already fallen, and man's spirit is already deadened. Now man lives in the soul and in the flesh; he lives by the soul and according to the flesh. Originally, man should have lived by and according to the spirit. But since the spirit of man is deadened, man lives by the soul and according to the flesh. Although sometimes the things he lives out appear to be good and nice, they are still lived out of the soul and the flesh and not out of the spirit. What is lived out by a fallen man, regardless of whether it is good or bad, is lived out by his "doing the desires of the flesh and of the thoughts" (Eph. 2:3). He has fallen into the soul and the flesh, and he also lives in his soul and his flesh. Therefore, he cannot contact God or serve God.

GOD'S SALVATION

The Bible shows us that because man has fallen into the flesh and lives in the flesh, if God wants to save man, He must save him out of the flesh. For this reason God Himself became flesh, and this God who became flesh was the Lord Jesus. He came to the place into which we have fallen. We have fallen into the flesh, so He came into the flesh. He came into the flesh to save us out of the flesh.

Although God prepared a body for us when He created us in the beginning, His intention was not for us to live according to the body and be controlled by the body. Rather, His intention was that we live according to the spirit. The body is just a vessel to contain the spirit. But since our spirit is deadened, we live according to the body and have fallen into the flesh. Therefore, God became flesh and came into the flesh to save us.

Although He became flesh, He Himself was Spirit. What He put on outwardly was the flesh, yet what He was inwardly was Spirit. The reason that He put on the flesh is that He might save us out of the flesh. The reason that He came as the Spirit is that He might save us into the spirit. Because of sin we have fallen from the spirit into the flesh. Through redemption He saved us from the flesh into the spirit. By His Spirit He put on our flesh and was put to death on the cross, on the one hand, crucifying and dealing with our flesh that we might be freed from our flesh, and on the other hand, through His resurrection, releasing and imparting Himself as the Spirit into us so that our spirit can be made alive and we can enter into our spirit.

Brothers and sisters, this is the center of God's salvation. God's salvation is to save us out of our flesh into our spirit.

The Lord Jesus became flesh and died on the cross in order to attain this goal. Through His death in the flesh He dealt with our flesh, and through His resurrection He imparted Himself as the Spirit into us. When we receive Him as our Savior, we receive Him as such a Savior. We do not merely receive Him as our Redeemer to deal with our sins, still less as a rabbi, a teacher, to teach us, as Nicodemus did. He did not come merely to solve the problem of sins for us, still less to teach us. Instead, He came to save us from our flesh and impart Himself as the Spirit into us to make our spirit alive. Of course, He also dealt with our sins, but this is only on the negative side. On the positive side, He came to impart Himself as the Spirit into us to save us from our flesh.

The salvation of God is absolutely not an outward teaching, nor is it only an objective redemption. In His salvation, on the one hand, God dealt with our flesh and, on the other hand, as the Spirit He entered into us, saving us and making us alive in our spirit. Therefore, God's salvation is to save us inwardly in our spirit, thereby causing us to be freed outwardly from our flesh. Such a salvation is very subjective to us.

We must not receive the Lord Jesus only as an objective Savior, a Savior who was put to death on the cross. We need to know that He came in order to impart Himself as the Spirit into us and enter into us as the Spirit. Therefore, we must also receive Him as a subjective Savior, a Savior who is in our spirit. He saves us not by teaching us or by correcting and adjusting us outwardly, as Nicodemus thought. Furthermore, He did not merely make redemption for our sins outwardly. Rather, He wants to come into us as the Spirit that we may be saved inwardly.

It is true that the Lord Jesus was once in the flesh outwardly and was able to be with man that man might receive His teaching, but even more as the Spirit He wanted to enter into man to enliven the spirit of man. It is true that in His crucifixion He bore our sins on the cross to solve the problem of sins for us, but even more He dealt with our flesh and released and imparted Himself as the Spirit into us. He wants to enliven our deadened spirit by Himself as the Spirit. He wants to be our Savior inwardly to save us from within.

MAN'S ERRONEOUS UNDERSTANDING

People always thought that the Lord's intention was to teach them or save them in an outward way. They knew the Lord outwardly and knew Him according to His outward doings. According to what the Lord was outwardly, Nicodemus regarded Him as a rabbi who came from God as a teacher to teach us. Many who saw the Lord casting out demons and healing the sick thought that He was the One who came particularly to heal them physically. Many who saw the Lord feeding the five thousand with five loaves and two fish thought that He came to do miracles to sustain them physically. The disciples who followed the Lord knew Him only outwardly as the Savior and the Christ; they did not know Him inwardly as God and the Father. They only knew and appreciated the fact that the Lord was with them outwardly. They did not know that the Lord wanted to enter into them and be with them. All their contacts with the Lord in those days were outward. They did not know that the Lord's intention was to enter into them that they might have a subjective and more intimate contact with the Lord within them. They hoped only that they would have the Lord's salvation and presence outwardly. They did not know that the Lord wanted to enter into them as the Spirit to be their salvation and to be with them. They knew Him only as a Savior outside of man; they did not know that He wanted to enter into man to be a Savior within man.

People always knew the Lord outwardly, thinking that the Lord's intention was merely to teach them, save them, heal them, and be with them outwardly as a Savior outside of them. People had this kind of understanding and consideration because they thought that their problems were merely outward. Nicodemus thought that his problem was that he lacked better teachings for his outward conduct, his outward behavior. Those who came to the Lord for healing thought that their problem was only their physical sickness. Those who came to the Lord to be fed with bread thought that their problem was their physical livelihood. The disciples who followed the Lord thought that their problem was that the Lord was going to leave them outwardly and that they were about to lose His outward presence, the presence of a visible Lord outwardly.

In the early days, all those who contacted the Lord and followed Him thought that man's problems are all outside of man. They thought that man needs to be taught, saved, healed, and cared for outwardly. They did not know that the problems of man are within him. Man needs to be saved and healed within. Nicodemus saw that his outward manner of life and his behavior were not good, but he did not realize that the life and the spirit within him were not good. Those who came to ask the Lord for healing saw that their outward body was sick, but they did not see that the spirit within them was deadened. Those who came to be fed with bread saw the need of their body outwardly, but they did not see the need of their spirit within. In those days the disciples saw the need for Christ outwardly; they did not see that they needed a Savior within them.

THE LORD'S LEADING IN REVELATION

Therefore, the Lord spent a considerable amount of effort to lead those who contacted Him and followed Him in those days to realize the problem and the need within them. The Lord showed Nicodemus that what he needed was not to be taught or corrected regarding his outward conduct or behavior, but to be born again in his spirit. No matter how much he was taught and corrected in his outward conduct or behavior, he still could not be saved inwardly. Only by being regenerated in his spirit could the spirit within him be made alive. His spirit was deadened, and he was living according to his soul and his flesh; his conduct and his behavior all were of his soul and his flesh. Since this was the case, no matter how he could be taught regarding his outward conduct and how he could be corrected in his outward behavior, his conduct and behavior would still be of the soul and the flesh. No matter how he could be taught and corrected, his spirit within him could not be enlivened within him, nor could his conduct or behavior be turned into a conduct or a behavior that is of the spirit. Therefore, the Lord showed Nicodemus that he needed to be regenerated in his spirit, that he needed to allow the Spirit to enter into his spirit that his spirit might be made alive. Then he could be of the spirit, could understand the spiritual things of God, and could participate in the kingdom of God.

The Lord expressed His distrust and displeasure with the crowds who came to Him for healing. They came to Him outwardly for the healing only of their body. They did not have the intention to receive Him within to be their Savior so that the spirit within them might be healed and saved. The Lord came that man might have the life of God and the Spirit of God so that the spirit of man might be made alive and man might be saved from within. Even when man came to Him outwardly and was healed physically, if he did not receive Him inwardly so that his spirit was made alive, then he still could live only in the flesh and not in the spirit, and he could live only according to the flesh and not according to the spirit, because his spirit was still dead. Therefore, if one only hopes to be healed outwardly and does not want to be saved inwardly, then the Lord cannot entrust Himself to him or be pleased with him.

To those who came to Him to eat of the bread and be filled, the Lord said, "Work not for the food which perishes, but for the food which abides unto eternal life" (John 6:27). He showed them that the food which perishes could sustain only their flesh but could not give life to their deadened spirit and make it alive. Only the words of life which He spoke to them were able to give life to their spirit and make it alive. They paid attention to nourishing and sustaining their outward flesh. However, the Lord told them that "the flesh profits nothing" (v. 63), that only the Spirit can give life to man and make man alive, and that the words of life which He spoke to them are spirit and are life. If they only outwardly received from Him the food for the body and did not inwardly receive His spiritual words of life, then the deadened spirit within them still did not have His life and was not made alive. The real need which they had and which the Lord would supply was not the outward food of the flesh but the inward spiritual life. The real problem which they had and which the Lord would solve for them was not how to sustain their outward flesh but how to enliven their inner spirit.

Furthermore, to the disciples who followed Him, the Lord showed them how He would enter into them as the Spirit that they might live with Him. Previously, while He was with them outwardly, they were able to receive some teachings, help, and consolation from Him outwardly, yet even more they needed to receive life and salvation within them. Therefore, He had to enter into them as the Spirit to be their life and salvation.

CONTACTING THE LORD FROM WITHIN

To those who contacted Him or followed Him, the Lord not only showed them their inner needs but also led them to contact Him and have dealings with Him inwardly. He showed Nicodemus that He is the One who is able to regenerate man, and then He led him to receive Him by exercising his faith inwardly. Previously, Nicodemus outwardly regarded Him only as a teacher who came from God; he did not know that in Him was the Spirit of God and the life of God. Therefore, he contacted the Lord outwardly merely according to his outward knowledge of Him. But the Lord showed Nicodemus that He had the Spirit of God and the life of God in Him and that if he would like to receive the divine Spirit and the divine life, then he must receive Him from within by exercising his faith. It seemed that He was saying to Nicodemus, "You are contacting Me outwardly to receive My teachings, but I don't want to teach you outwardly. You only see what is outside of Me, but you don't know what is inside of Me. I have the Spirit of God and the life of God within Me. I want to come into you that you may have the Spirit of God and the life of God. It is not good enough that you merely contact Me outwardly according to your sight. You still need to contact Me and receive Me within by faith; then you will receive the regeneration of the Holy Spirit and the life of God in your spirit. As the Spirit I will enter into your spirit. You must not only contact Me outwardly with your body, but you must contact Me with your spirit within. If you receive Me within by faith and contact Me with your spirit, I will enter into you as the Spirit that your spirit may receive the life of God."

Those who came to the Lord for healing only contacted the Lord with their body outwardly, but they did not contact Him inwardly with their spirit. Therefore, they could not please Him or be entrusted by Him. No one who merely contacts the Lord outwardly will be able to please Him and be entrusted by Him. Only by contacting Him with the spirit and receiving Him with the heart can one allow Him to accomplish what He wants to do in him, that is, to give him the life of God.

Those who came to Him to eat bread and be filled also contacted the Lord only outwardly with their body. But He showed them that it is in His words that He would impart the Spirit and life into man. If man wants to receive the Spirit and life, he must receive His words by exercising his faith within. The Lord is now the Spirit of life in resurrection, and the Spirit is embodied in His words for man to receive. But how can man receive His words? Man cannot use outward things to receive them; he can only use his faith within. Our words, which come from within us, are expressions of our inner being. The Lord's words are expressions of what He is within. He is Spirit and life within; hence, His words as His expressions are spirit and life. When man receives His words by faith within, man receives the Spirit and life. Therefore, in order to receive the Spirit and life, man must not merely contact Him outwardly; rather, man must contact Him inwardly. Although man cannot see the Spirit or life outwardly, he can believe His words inwardly. His words are spirit and are life. Therefore, when man receives His words inwardly by faith, the Spirit enters into man and touches the spirit of man, enlivening the spirit of man and causing man to have the life of God within.

Man knows only to contact the Lord outwardly and not inwardly. Not to mention others, even the disciples who followed Him in those days were also like this. They just wanted to see and touch Him outwardly. They knew only His outward doings and not His inward being. One day, one of the disciples, Philip, asked Him to show God to them. He was surprised and said to him, "Have I been so long a time with you, and you

have not known Me, Philip? He who has seen Me has seen the
Father;...I am in the Father and the Father is in Me" (John
14:8-11). They did not know what He was inwardly; they did
not know that inwardly He was God. Therefore, He made
known to them that God was in Him, that within He was
God, and that they should not just know Him and contact
Him according to what He was outwardly but even the more
according to what He is inwardly, thereby touching God, who
is in Him.

Furthermore, He told them later that He was going to ask
God to send the Holy Spirit. When the Holy Spirit would
come, He (the Lord) would enter into them as the Spirit to be
with them. He said that He was not leaving them as orphans
and that He was going away, but He was coming to them
(vv. 16-20). How did He go? He went to die on the cross. How
did He come? Through death and resurrection He became the
Spirit, and as the Spirit He entered into them. Therefore, on
the evening of the day of His resurrection He came into their
midst and breathed into them that they might receive the
Spirit. At that time they knew that He was in God, they were
in Him, and He was in them. Because He entered into them
as the Spirit, they then knew that He was in union with God,
they were in union with Him, and He was also in union with
them.

From that time—the evening of the day of the Lord's resurrection—the Lord led His disciples to know and appreciate
His presence within them. Previously He came into their
midst in his flesh to be with them outwardly. Now He wanted
to come into them as the Spirit to be with them inwardly.
Previously His presence with them was at specific moments,
was limited by time and space, and was visible. Now His
presence with them would be at every moment, would not be
limited by time or space, and would be invisible. Therefore,
since the evening of the day of His resurrection, every time
He came into their midst it was puzzling to them. The doors
of the room they were in were all shut tight, but suddenly He
came and stood in their midst. Then He went away without
their knowing how it happened. It seemed that His coming

and going were untraceable. It was always like this in all His dealings with them during the forty days after His resurrection. Once on the road to Emmaus, He drew near to the two disciples in a mysterious way and walked with them for a distance, but they did not recognize Him. It was not until they came to the village, entered into a house, and reclined at the table with Him that they recognized Him. But when they recognized Him, He suddenly disappeared again. It seemed that He came suddenly and went suddenly. In fact, it was not so; rather, it was that His presence with them was sometimes manifested and sometimes hidden. He dealt with them in this way to let them know that His presence with them now was different from before. His intention was to lead them to know that He was with them inwardly as the Spirit. He also wanted to train them to inwardly enjoy His constant presence, which is not limited by time and space, and thus learn to deal with Him and contact Him inwardly not by sight but by faith.

From the time of His resurrection, the Lord entered into His disciples as the Spirit to be with them. Although He later ascended to the heavens, He was still the Spirit indwelling His disciples to be with them. To this day it is still like this, and until He comes again it will be like this. Today He is sitting in the heavens, yet on the earth as the Spirit He enters into all those who contact Him by faith in spirit that He may be with them. This presence is not visible outwardly, but it can be sensed within. Today He cannot be seen outwardly, but He can be contacted in the spirit. When a person contacts Him by faith in the spirit, immediately he touches Him. Once a person receives Him within, immediately by His Spirit He enters into him, not into his mind, emotion, or will, but into his spirit.

THE SPIRIT BEING MADE ALIVE

Once He enters into the spirit of man, He makes it alive. A person is saved when the Lord enters into him as the Spirit imparting His life—the life of God—into him and thus enlivening his deadened spirit. This is what man needs today, and this is also what the Lord wants to do today. The spirit within man has been deadened, and man has fallen into the soul and the flesh. Now what man needs is for the spirit within him to be made alive. This cannot be accomplished by outward teachings and improvements. No matter how you try to teach his soul or improve his flesh outwardly, you cannot cause the spirit within him to be made alive. This is just like the electric fan. If it is short of electricity within, any repair or assistance you render outwardly is useless. The so-called sages all taught people how to cultivate and reform themselves outwardly. Their outward teachings and improvements cannot cause the spirit within man to be made alive, just as the repairs done outwardly to an electric fan that is short of electricity cannot cause the fan to be supplied with electricity within. No outward method, be it ethics, education, or even religion, can be of help to the deadened spirit within man. Only the Lord of life, the One in whom is life and in whom is resurrection, who enters into man as the Spirit can cause the deadened spirit to have life and be made alive.

The way of the Lord's salvation does not start from the outside. It does not correct and control man outwardly as ethical teachings and educational instructions do. The way of the Lord's salvation starts from within man, from the deepest part of man, which is the spirit within man, by imparting His life to it and making it alive. As the Spirit He enters into man's spirit and thus causes it to be saved. When the Spirit enters into man and contacts the spirit of man, the spirit of man is made alive. When the spirit of man is made alive, man is able to know God and to serve God. Furthermore, when the spirit of man is made alive, man delights in serving and worshipping God. Once our spirit is made alive due to the entrance of the Lord as the Spirit, it then has the nature of knowing God, serving God, and worshipping God, and it has the desire and the ability to know God, serve God, and worship God. Previously, because our spirit was deadened and we lived according to our soul and our flesh, we were neither willing nor able to serve God. Now since our spirit has been made alive, we live according to the spirit and therefore we are willing and able to serve God.

CHAPTER THREE

ONLY THE SPIRIT
BEING ABLE TO CONTACT GOD

Scripture Reading: John 3:6; 6:63; Phil. 3:3; Rom. 8:6

In the two previous chapters we saw that all the service that God wants from man must be in spirit. To enable us to serve Him in spirit, He became the Spirit through incarnation, death, and resurrection. Then as the Spirit He comes to contact us in our spirit, making our deadened spirit alive so that we can serve Him by contacting Him as the Spirit in our enlivened spirit. Only the service that comes out of the contact and fellowship of our spirit with the Spirit is the service that God wants, and only this kind of service is acceptable to Him. This is how God wants us to worship Him—in spirit.

TWO DIFFERENT SOURCES

The verses above show us that in the matter of service to God there are two different sources: one is the flesh and the other is the Spirit. John 3:6 says, "That which is born of the flesh is flesh, and that which is born of the Spirit is spirit." This shows us two different sources issuing in two different results. One source is the flesh, and the other source is the Spirit. Of course, the kind of result produced is determined by the kind of source that produces it. That which is born of the flesh can only be flesh and can never be spirit. That which is born of the Spirit can never be flesh but can only be spirit.

John 6:63 says, "It is the Spirit who gives life; the flesh profits nothing." Since the Spirit and the flesh are different sources, they have different natures. Consequently, their capabilities are also different. The substance of the Spirit (the

Spirit of God) is the life of God; therefore, the Spirit gives life. The substance of the flesh is vanity and equals nothing; therefore, the flesh profits nothing.

Romans 8:6 says, "For the mind set on the flesh is death, but the mind set on the spirit is life and peace." The flesh not only profits nothing but also results in death, while the Spirit not only gives life but also imparts peace. The result of our serving God by the flesh is "nothing" and "death"; whereas the result of our serving God by the Spirit is "life" and "peace."

Notwithstanding, Philippians 3:3 shows that just as we have the possibility of serving God by the spirit, so we have the possibility of serving by the flesh. Moreover, the possibility of serving by the flesh is very great in those of us who have not thoroughly dealt with the flesh and whose spirit has not yet become mature. Formerly we were deadened in our spirit, we had fallen into the flesh, and we were living by the flesh. Now, although our spirit has been made alive through God's salvation, we are still living in the flesh. Our spirit has not become mature yet and it is not strong enough. Furthermore, perhaps due to our ignorance concerning spiritual matters we may not even know that we must serve God by the spirit and not by the flesh. Therefore, after we have been saved, in the same way that we conduct ourselves, we serve God mostly by the flesh and very little by, of, and in the spirit.

Many people think that our flesh is capable only of committing sins but not capable of serving God, that we are likely to commit sins but not likely to serve God by our flesh. In their consideration, there is only such a thing as man committing sin by the flesh, but not such a thing as man serving God by the flesh. However, the Bible tells us that just as man commits sins by the flesh, so man can also serve God by the flesh. Not only so, the facts also show that many indeed serve God by the flesh just as they commit sins by the flesh. No doubt the apostle Paul served God by the flesh before he was saved (Acts 22:3; Phil. 3:4-7). Although many Christians have been saved, they still serve God by the flesh, just as the apostle Paul did before he was saved.

There are some others who think that using the flesh to commit sins is wrong, but using the flesh to serve God is right, and that committing sins by the flesh is forbidden, but serving God by the flesh is permissible. They do not realize, however, that when one serves God by the flesh, not only is his service unacceptable to God, but it is also virtually impossible for him to have access to God and to contact God, because the flesh simply cannot have access to God, nor can it touch God.

The flesh includes man's fallen body and soul. Originally, man was spiritual, being dominated by the spirit. After the spirit became dead due to man's fall, the soul rose up, replacing the spirit to control man and subjected itself to the lusts of the human body. The human body became the flesh due to its lusts, the sin derived from Satan. Since the human soul is in subjection to the lusts of the body, it becomes fleshly. Therefore, in the Scriptures *flesh* denotes all the soulish and fleshly things outside of the spirit. (It also frequently denotes the soulish and fleshly man.) All things outside of the spirit are the flesh. To serve God by anything outside of the spirit is to serve God by the flesh. This kind of service is of no effect.

CONTACTING GOD ONLY BY BEING IN SPIRIT

We have already seen that God is Spirit and therefore He created man with a spirit that man may serve Him in spirit. Moreover, in His salvation He comes to contact man as the Spirit. Therefore, when we serve Him, we must contact the Spirit in our spirit. Unless a person's spirit is touched by the Spirit of God, he cannot know God, serve God, or contact God. The service that God wants from man is a service that is in the spirit of man. And the contact that God wants to have with man is a contact that is in the Spirit of God and in the spirit of man. Therefore, if someone wants to serve God, he must touch the Spirit of God in his spirit, he must be contacted by the Spirit of God in his spirit, and the two spirits—his spirit and God's Spirit—must have mutual fellowship and be mutually joined. Only then will he be able to contact God and serve God. Only such a one is able to know God and understand the things of God. No one can understand the things of God unless he touches the Spirit of God in his spirit. This may be compared to someone trying to touch colors without using his eyes or catch a sound without using his ears, which is impossible. Unless a person's spirit is touched by the Holy Spirit, he has no way to understand the things of God and thus he cannot serve God.

NOT USING THE BODY TO CONTACT GOD

Therefore, we must see clearly which part of our being we should use to serve God. We can contact God only by the spirit and not by the body. Our spirit can feel God, but our body cannot. None of the parts and organs of our physical body is able to feel or sense God. Many new ones expect to see God with their eyes, to touch God with their hands, or to sense God with a certain part of their body; this is impossible because God cannot be contacted by us in our body.

Before they begin praying to God, some have the concept that God will come upon their body while they are praying and that their body will be feverish and trembling. Before they pray, they are prepared for their body to be feverish and trembling, and after they have prayed, if they are neither feverish nor trembling, they think that God is not real. It is wrong for them to have the concept that God will come upon their body and to prepare themselves to touch God with their body. Man cannot touch God with his body because this is not what God wants. If someone always expects to feel God with his body, the result will be that the demons, not God, will come upon his body. The demons, the evil spirits of Satan, cling to the human body. However, the Holy Spirit of God is not like that. The Holy Spirit comes into the spirit of man, but the unclean spirits cling to man's physical body. This is a great difference. If a man tries to use the body to contact God, he may end up contacting the evil spirits. This is neither proper nor permissible.

NOT USING THE SOUL TO CONTACT GOD

Man cannot use his body to contact God; likewise, he cannot use his soul to contact God. Like the human body, the human soul cannot be connected with God. None of the parts of the soul, whether the mind, the emotion, or the will, can reach God, know God, or contact God. Yet today man always tries to use the mind to consider God, understand God, and comprehend God. When he hears about God, he considers that perhaps God is like this or like that. Man's knowledge of God is mostly the imaginations of his intellect, the mind in man's soul. As a result, man's knowledge of God consists mostly of illusions and vain things. This is because the human intellect (mind) cannot contact or touch God, nor can the human thought know and comprehend God. Man's intellect, the mind in man's soul, is not the faculty for contacting and receiving God.

Some have believed in the Lord by believing the doctrines of the Bible with their mind instead of receiving the Lord with their spirit. I have met many people like this. If you ask them whether they have believed in the Lord, they answer firmly that they have. If you ask them further whether they are saved, they will recite to you Ephesians 2:8: "For by grace you have been saved through faith." If you ask them whether they have eternal life, they will recite John 3:16: "Every one who believes into Him would not perish, but would have eternal life." However, if you question them as to whether they are truly saved and have eternal life, they do not have the assurance and they dare not say so. This is because they do not have the experience of salvation. Although they have the scriptural doctrines in their mind, they still do not have the Lord in their spirit. They have only received the scriptural doctrines in their mind; they have not yet experienced the Lord's salvation in their spirit.

When listening to a message, many people use only their mind and not their spirit. As a result, while their mind touches the message, their spirit fails to touch God. Their spirit is neither moved nor dealt with by the Spirit of God, in spite of the fact that their mind is affected and taught by the message. It is even possible for one's mind to very clearly know and thoroughly understand the message and yet his spirit does not touch God even a little. His mind is filled with the message, but his spirit is still void of God. God's word may enter into man's mind through man's understanding, but God Himself can enter into man's spirit only through the Spirit.

Many brothers and sisters also use only their mind and not their spirit in reading the Bible. Hence, they cannot receive inspiration from the Bible nor can they touch God in their spirit through the reading of the Scriptures. Their mind can clearly study many doctrines, and their thoughts can figure out many truths. Nevertheless, their spirit has not been touched by God in His word, and therefore they have not received the supply of God's life. They have not been moved, strengthened, enlightened, or cleansed in their spirit by God as the Spirit through His word.

Many brothers and sisters also use only their mind and not their spirit when they pray. In their regular morning and evening prayers, they recite the same things from their mind as if they were reciting from a book. They recite something first concerning themselves and then concerning their family, the church, the nation, and the world. Their recitation starts from themselves and covers the whole world. Every day when they pray, they recite once in this manner, and if they cannot finish it in the morning, they make it up in the evening. For a few days in the beginning, this kind of recitation has a good taste to them, but after a longer period of time, it begins to feel burdensome. Yet at the same time it has become a habit, so they have no peace if they do not recite. This kind of praying with the mind according to a set form cannot enable a person to contact God in the spirit, nor can it enable him to touch the presence of God and receive the supply of God. It only causes his heart to feel burdened and his spirit to be dry and empty, without being watered or satisfied.

Very often when the brothers call a hymn or offer a prayer in the meeting, they do it with their mind and not with their spirit. The hymns they select come from the considerations in their mind based on certain needs and not from being moved in their spirit. Moreover, the prayers they offer are prayers composed with their mind according to the existing situation and are not prayers released from their spirit. Therefore, the hymns they call and the prayers they offer cannot touch God, nor can they touch the spirit of others to make them sense God in their spirit and to uplift their spirit.

Many even preach the word with their mind instead of their spirit. Prior to their preaching, they first consider and select a topic, and then they use their mind to arrange the sections, prepare some stories, and add some illustrations. Then at the time of preaching, they speak the preconceived message in a very good order from their mind according to their memory. This kind of preaching is altogether done by using the human mind and depending on human thoughts. It is no wonder that it cannot bring the audience into contact with God, nor can it cause them to be moved by God. Furthermore, even the speaker himself is unable to touch God or be moved by God.

Even in visitation and in contacting people in spiritual matters, many brothers and sisters also merely use their mind and not their spirit. When they talk to people about the gospel or about spiritual matters, they do it according to the truth which they have comprehended in their understanding and the doctrine which they have remembered in their mind, instead of doing it according to the inspiration and revelation which they have received in their spirit. Therefore, their word can neither release forth God nor move the spirit within the listener. Likewise, their visitation cannot impart God and God's supply to others to solve their spiritual problems.

Concerning all these spiritual matters, matters that pertain to the service of God, if a person touches any of these things merely with his mind and not with his spirit, he will not be able to touch or gain God, nor will he be able to touch God's life or God's supply.

Just as the mind in man's soul cannot contact God, so the emotion and will in man's soul also cannot contact God. A person's emotion might be moved and his will might be changed, yet it is possible that he still has not contacted God. Very often, when someone listens to messages, reads the Scriptures, prays, attends meetings, or receives exhortation and instruction, his emotions may be greatly moved and because of this his will may also have a great change so that he strongly decides to turn to God and to live for God. Yet he may not have touched or contacted God at all. This is due to the fact that although his emotion and his will have been moved by the spiritual things, his spirit has not been moved by God. Spiritual matters may move his emotion and his will, but God wants to move and touch his spirit. His emotion and his will can contact the spiritual things but they cannot contact God.

ONLY USING THE SPIRIT

We must be clear and remember that God is Spirit and that only the spirit can touch and contact the Spirit. Therefore, if we want to contact and touch God in any matter, we must use our spirit. Apart from our spirit, we cannot touch God in any spiritual matter. A certain matter may be very spiritual, but if we do not use our spirit to contact God in that matter, we simply cannot touch God. A spiritual matter in itself still cannot enable us to touch God. We still must use our spirit to contact God in that spiritual matter; only then can we touch God.

When a person believes in the Lord, it is not enough that he receives the truth of the gospel merely with his mind. He must also receive the Lord with his spirit. Man's mind can only contact the truth; it cannot contact the Lord. If a person merely touches the truth and does not contact the Lord, he cannot be saved. He can receive the Lord's salvation only by contacting the Lord. However, in order to contact the Lord he must use his spirit. He has to go beyond and deeper than his mind and get into the spirit deep within him to be enlightened and moved by the Holy Spirit, to be conscious of his sins, to confess that he is a sinner, and to receive the crucified and resurrected Christ, the ever-living Savior, not a dead doctrine. Only then can he touch the Spirit of the Lord, that is, contact the Lord Himself and receive the Lord's salvation.

This is very different from someone who receives the doctrine of the gospel merely in his mind. One person who understands and comprehends with his mind takes doctrine as his goal, whereas another person who is moved and who receives salvation in his spirit takes Christ as his object. In the former case, someone may understand and receive many doctrines in his mind without touching Christ. In the latter case, the other person can contact Christ in his spirit without knowing many doctrines. In the former case, he may receive a doctrinal teaching and obtain some doctrinal knowledge, but his spirit may not be saved by Christ with His life. In the latter case, this one is enlightened by the Holy Spirit and is regenerated in his spirit, even though he may not understand many of the gospel truths or obtain a great deal of gospel knowledge.

A person may know many doctrines but may not receive the Lord's salvation. He may have the knowledge of sin in his mind but not have the consciousness of sin in his spirit. In his mind he knows he is sinful, but in his spirit he does not feel so. He may have understood and comprehended Christ in his mind, but in his spirit he has not yet contacted or touched Christ. The reason for this is that he uses his mind to study the doctrines about Christ instead of using his spirit to contact Christ Himself. If he is willing to contact Christ with his spirit, and if he is willing to be moved by the Holy Spirit in his spirit to contact Christ and receive Christ, he will be able to touch Christ and gain Christ in his spirit. Thus, he will be able to receive Christ's salvation of life and experience a change from within his spirit to his outward being.

When a person listens to a message, he must also go beyond and deeper than the mind, emotion, and will of his soul and get into his spirit to be inspired by God and to contact Christ Himself. If he merely uses his mind, emotion, and will to listen to the message, he can only understand its meaning in his mind, receive its inspiration in his emotion, and make a decision because of it in his will. He can only contact the message itself by the mind, emotion, and will; he cannot touch the Christ in the message. The message itself, which is merely letter and knowledge, cannot afford man the salvation of life or the spiritual supply. Only Christ in the message is life and Spirit, and only He can give life and spiritual reality to man. Man may contact the message itself with his mind, emotion, and will, but to contact the Christ in the message he has to seek Christ, look to Christ, draw nigh to Christ, and worship Christ with his spirit. In this way he can contact Him and have fellowship with Him.

When a person reads the Bible, he must use his concentrated and focused mind to study and meditate, but even the more he must use a quiet and eager spirit to seek God and His revelation through the word of God—the holy Bible—and thus receive His enlightenment and supply. The mind can only understand the letters of the Bible and comprehend its doctrines; the mind cannot contact the God revealed in it or receive the life spoken of therein. Only the spirit can contact God and receive life through understanding the Bible and comprehending the truths by the mind. Therefore, when we read the Scriptures, we must draw near to God, contact God, and have fellowship with God in our spirit through His word. Only then will we be able to touch and gain Him and to receive spiritual enlightenment and life supply.

When a person prays, even the more he needs to use the spirit and to be in the spirit. Although the Bible says that we should pray also with the understanding (the mind), it does not mean that we pray only with the understanding. Rather, it means that we should use the understanding to comprehend the burden and feeling in the spirit and then pray with words from the understanding to express the burden and feeling in the spirit. If we pray only with the understanding, with the mind, with the intellect, we can neither receive inspiration nor sense God's presence. We must pray with the spirit and in the spirit, and we must have the burden and the sense in the spirit. Then we must use the understanding to pray and express the burden and the sense in the spirit. Only then can we touch God and His presence and receive the watering and supply of the Spirit.

Someone may ask, What is it to pray with the mind, and what is it to pray with the spirit? To pray with the mind is to pray according to what the mind remembers and thinks, without any feeling in the spirit. Many times we first decide on what to pray and then we exercise our memory to pray with our mind according to what we have already decided. Sometimes we may have decided what to pray, but when we pray, we always use our mind to think, and even contemplate, about what to pray, and then we pray according to what we have thought and contemplated. We often have a list of things or a set form of prayer which we pray by reciting. Also, we often merely pray according to a record or report of the items for prayer by repeating the items once. All such prayers are prayers by the mind and not by the spirit. These kinds of prayers are merely from our mind and come out through our mouth without any inspiration. Such prayers not only are unable to move God and others, but they cannot even move ourselves, because they are not the living inspiration from the spirit but the dead knowledge from the mind.

Praying with the spirit is different. Although praying with the spirit also requires using the mind, the mind is not the source of prayer but merely a faculty through which prayer passes. When a person prays by using the spirit, his prayer does not originate from the mind. Rather, it originates from the spirit and passes through the mind. Instead of praying according to what he remembers and considers in the mind, he prays according to the sense and burden in the spirit. However, he uses the mind to understand the sense and burden in the spirit and expresses such understanding in prayer. Since sometimes there is first the knowledge and memory in the mind and then prayer, it seems that the prayer is according to what the mind knows and remembers. Actually, however, the knowledge and memory in the mind have already become the feeling and burden in the spirit. One must first have the feeling and burden in the spirit, and then he uses his mind, his understanding, to express in prayer the feeling and burden of the spirit. This is to pray with the spirit. This kind of prayer requires a person to go beyond, go deeper than, his mind, emotion, and will that he may contact the Spirit of God in his spirit to receive the sense and burden of the spirit. This kind of prayer is according to divine inspiration and not according to a set form. It is fresh and not stale. It enables the praying one to touch God and sense His presence, and at the same time it also causes the praying one himself as well as those who hear him to be moved, watered, and supplied by the Spirit.

Very often this kind of praying in the spirit was not in one's original consideration. For example, someone originally intended to pray for his job, his health, or his family, including his children. But when he comes to the presence of God, the Spirit of God touches his spirit and causes him to feel that he is full of shortcomings before God. At this moment the feeling and burden in his spirit are his shortcomings. Therefore, he no longer cares to pray for his job, his health, or his family. Instead, he just follows the feeling in his spirit to confess to God all his shortcomings before Him in order to relieve the burden in his spirit. This kind of prayer enables him to touch God, to enter deeper into God, to have fellowship with God, to be more filled by God, and to receive the sweet nourishing and rich supply of God. If he would be willing to disregard the matters which he has remembered and has prepared to pray, and instead would just pay attention to the feeling in his spirit and keep on praying according to that feeling, then within him he will receive the unlimited spiritual blessing of God. He will feel joyful, peaceful, at ease, satisfied, fresh, shining, living, and strong. After praying, not only he himself feels that he is full of the presence of God, but even those who contact him will feel that there is an unexplainable condition and power upon him.

Therefore, brothers and sisters, when we pray, we must first have the sense and burden from God by contacting Him with our spirit and touching Him in our spirit, and then we must use our understanding, our mind, to express the sense and burden in our spirit with words of prayer. When we pray, we must first reject the memory and thoughts in our mind and then draw near to God in our spirit to touch His feeling and receive His burden. This does not mean that we should not bring the things in our memory before God in prayer. What it means is that all the matters for which we intend to pray must first become the feeling and burden we have from God in our spirit, and then they can become the prayers that we ought to have before God. Therefore, when we bring a certain matter before God in prayer, instead of praying at once for that matter from our mind, we should first contact God in the spirit to touch His feeling. If that matter becomes the feeling in our spirit before God, then we may pray for it. Otherwise, we should not pray for it even though we have already decided to pray for it originally. If, without any feeling in our spirit, we still pray for it, then we are praying according to our mind and with our mind. Thus, we surely will not be able to touch God and His presence, because we are in our mind uttering a prayer of the mind. Only when we pray for a certain matter that has become the feeling and burden in our spirit can we touch the presence of God and be watered by Him.

Recently when I was in Manila, a brother asked me, "What is a prayer of the mind? And what is a prayer of the spirit?" Although I felt it is not easy to explain, I was able to answer him with a simple sentence. A prayer of the mind comes out of thinking, whereas a prayer of the spirit comes out of feeling. Any prayer that comes out of our thought is a prayer of the mind because it comes out of the mind. Any prayer that is uttered out of the feeling deep within us is a prayer of the spirit because it comes out of the spirit. We should pray for many matters, but we should not pray merely according to what we remember and consider in our mind. Every matter for prayer must first become the feeling and burden in our spirit before God. We must pray only according to the feeling in our spirit and for the burden in our spirit because we can only pray by contacting God in our spirit. We may bring many things before God, but we must see whether God makes them the feelings and burdens in our spirit before we decide whether we should pray for them. We can pray only for the matters with which we have been inspired; we can pray only by touching God in our inspiration; and we can pray only in our inspiration the prayers that touch God.

In our prayers we should follow the feeling in our spirit not only when we petition God but even when we praise and thank God. We should not praise and thank God merely according to the doctrines, knowledge, or sentiments concerning some outward things. Otherwise, although our praises and thanksgivings are toward God, they are of the letter, formal, outward, of the mind, not in the spirit, and without the Spirit. Only the praises and thanksgivings which are according to the feeling in our spirit can enable us to touch God and to have the confirmation of God's acceptance, the feeling of the presence of God which He gives us in our spirit. This is because this kind of prayer is in the spirit and is full of the Spirit.

When one leads a meeting, whether he chooses a hymn, prays, speaks, or testifies, he should be in the spirit and act according to the feeling in the spirit. In many instances, the activities in the meeting are carried out merely according to rules, common sense, or certain needs. These activities are all done according to one's mind or emotion, instead of being done in one's spirit according to the sense in the spirit. Therefore, they are ritualistic, formal, intellectual, rational, and emotional. They cannot cause people to sense the presence of God or receive the supply of God. In the meeting, before one does anything, he must open his spirit to God to contact God and have fellowship with God in his spirit that he may receive inspiration from God. Then what he does will enable others to sense God's presence and receive God's supply. All the activities in the meeting must be initiated in the spirit in this way. For example, when a person chooses a hymn in the meeting, he must not choose one just at the right time, for the right situation, and with the right subject merely according to his knowledge of the hymns or according to his understanding of which kind of hymn is needed for which kind of meeting. Rather, he must also use his spirit to sense the spirit of the meeting and to receive inspiration from God concerning a certain point, and then select a hymn that can express, release, and touch that inspiration. As another example, when one speaks or testifies in the meeting, he must also not do it merely according to the outward situation and need by speaking a word that fits the situation or giving a testimony that meets the need. Rather, he still must use his spirit to touch God's feeling concerning that situation and need and to receive inspiration from God, and then express something according to the sense in his spirit. It is not enough merely to have the knowledge about meetings in the mind. There is still the need to touch the feeling of God and receive His inspiration by fellowshipping and contacting Him in the spirit. Only in this way can others sense life and reality in their spirit. Otherwise, they can only sense death and vanity.

It is the same when a person preaches the word. He must not preach a word that fits the situation and meets the need merely based upon his doctrinal knowledge and according to the outward situation and need. If he does this, the word he preaches is merely of the knowledge, of the letter, of the mind, and not in the spirit. To preach the word in the spirit, a person must be in his spirit and touch the feeling of God to receive the inspiration from God concerning that particular situation and that particular need. Then he can release the feeling in his spirit with the appropriate doctrine and word. Only by such preaching can the speaker himself touch God's presence and receive God's supply and the listeners also receive the edification in life and obtain the spiritual help.

Even when we go to visit others, we must contact them in our spirit and according to the feeling in our spirit. We must not speak to them merely according to the doctrines which we have understood and remembered in our mind or according to their outward condition and needs. Otherwise, we will not be able to bring him to God, nor will we be able to impart God to him to supply the need in his spirit or deal with the problem in his spirit. When we touch God in our spirit and contact others out of the sense of God's presence, we enable others to touch God and gain God, and we also enable them to receive the spiritual enlightenment and comfort, as well as the supply of life and edification, in their spirit. Only by contacting others in the spirit with the presence of God can we touch the Spirit of God and also touch the spirit of others. Moreover, only by this can others touch the Spirit of God with their spirit and receive the supply and help from the Spirit of God in their spirit.

Therefore, in our service to God, regardless of what we do, we must always use our spirit and be in our spirit. Only then can we touch God. This is a great law in the universe. This law is that man must use his human spirit and be in his human spirit to contact God. To contact God, man must do it according to this law and by fulfilling this law. Anyone who contacts God not according to this law violates God's ordination and therefore cannot touch God. Because God is Spirit, anyone who wants to contact Him must use his spirit and be in his spirit. Only the spirit can touch the Spirit; therefore, only the spirit can touch God.

CHAPTER FOUR

THE SENSE OF THE SPIRIT AND KNOWING THE SPIRIT

Scripture Reading: Rom. 8:2, 6

We have already seen three points: First, God is Spirit, and those who worship and serve Him must be in spirit; second, ultimately God comes into our spirit as the Spirit to receive our service to Him; and third, we can contact God only in the spirit.

HOW TO KNOW THE SPIRIT

In this chapter we will look at a fourth point, which is how to know the spirit. I believe that, after listening to the previous three messages, many brothers and sisters naturally will have such questions as: What really is this thing called the spirit? How can we know the spirit? And how can we touch the spirit? I admit that such questions are not easy to answer. To explain what the spirit is like is rather difficult. To speak of the body is very easy, because we can see it and touch it. To speak of the soul is also not difficult, because though the soul is abstract, we can feel it and know it by its functions and actions, such as thinking, considering, determining, decision-making, and being pleased, angry, sorrowful, and joyful. Only when we speak of the spirit is it truly difficult. To speak about the spirit is not easy; even to understand the spirit is not easy. Nevertheless, we will attempt to speak of it. We can know the spirit through four things.

FOUR THINGS

Romans 8 speaks of the spirit. It is difficult to find another place in the Bible which speaks of our condition in the spirit as clearly as this one. Therefore, if we want to know the spirit, it is imperative that we pay attention to this passage. In speaking of the spirit, the apostle uses four things.

The first thing is life. In verse 2 he refers to "the Spirit of life." In so doing he shows us that the Spirit he speaks of here is the Spirit of life, the Spirit which is related to life, contains life, and belongs to life. Then in verse 6 he says that "the mind set on the spirit is life." This means that life is the issue of the spirit, and the spirit is the source of life; therefore, by touching the spirit we touch life. Life and the spirit are mutually related; hence, we can know the spirit through life. Although it may be difficult to know the spirit, it is relatively easy to apprehend life.

The second thing is law. In verse 2 the apostle speaks not only of "the Spirit of life" but even of "the law of the Spirit of life." This tells us that the Spirit he speaks of here not only belongs to life but also has a law. Therefore, when he speaks of the Spirit, he speaks of life, and he speaks likewise of the law. He joins the three—life, Spirit, and law—together. Life and the Spirit cannot be separated; law and the Spirit likewise cannot be divided. Life is the content and issue of the Spirit, whereas law is the function and action of the Spirit. By contacting life we touch the spirit; by sensing the law we also sense the spirit. Though the spirit is hard to find, the law is not difficult to seek. Therefore, by the law we can find the spirit.

The third thing is peace. In verse 6 the apostle says that "the mind set on the spirit is life and peace." This means that the result of setting the mind on the spirit is not only life but also peace. Therefore, life is the issue of the spirit, and peace is also the issue of the spirit. When we touch the spirit, we touch life and we likewise touch peace. Just as life can make us apprehend the spirit, so also peace can cause us to realize the spirit.

The fourth thing is death. In verse 6, before the apostle says that "the mind set on the spirit is life and peace," he says that "the mind set on the flesh is death." Here he uses something negative to bring forth by contrast the positive. Flesh and spirit are opposites, and so are death and life. Life is the issue of the spirit and is derived from the spirit. Death is the issue of the flesh and is derived from the flesh. Life causes us to know the things derived from the spirit, thus enabling us to know the spirit from the positive side. Death causes us to know the matters derived from the flesh, thus unveiling the spirit from the negative side. Therefore, just as life enables us to know the spirit from the positive side, so death also enables us to understand the spirit from the negative side. To know the spirit we need to know life, and we need to understand the opposite of life, which is death.

Thus, according to what the apostle says regarding these four things—life, law, peace, and death—we see that they are closely related to the spirit both positively and negatively. If we thoroughly understand these four things, we can clearly know the spirit, which is decidedly related to them.

HAVING CONSCIOUSNESS

All these four things contain or convey a certain kind of consciousness. Except for the lowest plant life, every life definitely has a certain consciousness. The higher the life, the richer is its consciousness. The life of the Spirit of life spoken of here is the life of God Himself, which is the highest life; therefore, it is the richest in consciousness. This life within us causes us to be full of spiritual consciousness, enabling us to sense the spirit and the things of the spirit.

Although the law of an unconscious object does not belong to the realm of consciousness, the law of a conscious life does belong to the realm of consciousness. For example, if I hit a brother, he immediately feels pain; if I stretch out my hand toward his eyes, his eyelids immediately blink. He reacts in this way because in his body there is the law of life which compels him to do so. The moment I strike him, he feels pain—this is a law. The moment I stretch out my hand toward him, his eyes blink—this is also a law. Though these are laws, if you ask him what they are, he will say they are a matter of consciousness. This proves that the law of the physical life belongs to the order of consciousness. Since the life of the Spirit of life is the life of God, which is rich in consciousness, the law of the Spirit of life naturally is also full of consciousness.

The peace spoken of here is, of course, the peace within us. The peace within is entirely a matter of consciousness. It is not likely that we could have peace within and yet not feel it. Therefore, the peace spoken of here is also a matter of consciousness.

Moreover, even the death spoken of here is a matter of consciousness. Death causes man to lose his consciousness. When a man dies, he loses his consciousness. Therefore, when a man has no consciousness, it is proof that within him there is the working of death; though he may not have died completely, he is nearly dead.

Furthermore, in spiritual matters, death causes us not only to lose the sense of life but also to have the sense of death. When we set our mind on the flesh, death becomes active in us. On the one hand, it causes us to lose the sense of life within, and on the other hand, it causes us to have the sense of uneasiness, discomfort, depression, and oppression. This kind of uneasy, uncomfortable, depressed, and oppressed feeling is the sense of death and causes us to sense death.

Thus, these four—life, law, peace, and death—all have a consciousness related to them. The consciousness of these things enables us to touch the sense of the spirit and thereby know the spirit. Therefore, we should spend some time to examine the consciousness of these four things.

THE SENSE OF LIFE

Let us first look at the sense of life. The life spoken of here is the life of the Spirit of life. Therefore, this life is of the Spirit, from the Spirit, and rests with the Spirit. The Spirit with which this life rests is not only the Spirit of God but also our spirit. This Spirit is the Spirit of God *and* our spirit mingled as one spirit. In the Old Testament time, the Spirit of God only fell upon men, so that men received the power of God from without. He did not enter into man so that man could receive the life of God from within. Thus, in Old Testament times the Spirit of God was only the Spirit of power; He was not yet the Spirit of life. Not until the time of the New Testament did the Spirit of God enter into man as the Spirit of life so that man received the life of God from within. Today in the New Testament time, the Spirit of God is not only the Spirit of power but also the Spirit of life. He not only descends upon man, causing man to obtain the power of God outwardly, and He not only moves man, convicting man and causing man to confess, repent, and believe in the Lord. He further enters into man so that man may have the life of God inwardly, and He also dwells within man as the Spirit of life. When upon being moved by Him, we repent, believe, and receive the Lord Jesus as our Savior, He then enters into us and puts the life of God in us. At this time He enters into us as the Spirit of life, the Spirit of the life of God. The life of God is in Him; thus, He is the life of God. Therefore, when He enters into us, the life of God enters into us. He enters into us with the life of God as the *Spirit* of life. When He enters, He enters into *our spirit,* not into our mind, emotion, or will. He enters into our *spirit,* puts the life of God in our *spirit,* and dwells in our *spirit.* Thus, the Spirit of life is mingled together with our spirit. Now, the Spirit of God together with the life of God (He is the life of God itself) dwells in our spirit, so that the three—He Himself, the life of God, and our spirit—may be mingled as one and never be separated.

We may use an illustration of a glass which originally had plain water within it. We can blend into it some concentrated fruit juice that contains sugar, so that it becomes a glass of sugar-juice-water, a three-in-one drink. The water signifies our spirit, the fruit juice concentrate represents the Spirit of God, and the sugar stands for the life of God. The Spirit of God containing the life of God mingles with our spirit, thus making these three—the Spirit of God, the life of God, and our spirit—a three-in-one spirit of life. This is what Romans 8:2 speaks of.

Thus, the spirit, in which rests the life of the Spirit of life of which we are speaking, includes the Spirit of God and our spirit. It is a spirit which is a mingling of the Spirit of God with our spirit. Bible translators have understood the Spirit mentioned in Romans 8 as the Holy Spirit. Therefore, they have written *Spirit* with a capital *S.* Many readers of the Bible have also thought that the Spirit mentioned here refers only to the Holy Spirit. Yet spiritual fact and spiritual experience tell us that the Spirit mentioned here is the mingling of the Holy Spirit with our spirit. In verse 16 of this chapter the apostle sets forth this spiritual fact, which is also our spiritual experience. He says, "The Spirit Himself witnesses with our spirit." By speaking in this manner, he clearly tells us that the spirit he mentioned before is the one spirit, which is the mingling of "the Spirit...with our spirit." To say that this spirit is the Holy Spirit is all right, and to say that it is our spirit is also not wrong. It is like the water in the glass with concentrated fruit juice. You may say that it is fruit juice, and you may also say it is water. This is because the two have become mingled as one. Likewise, the Holy Spirit and our spirit are also mingled as one spirit. Within this one spirit, which is the mingling of the two, there is the life which God bestows on us. Thus, it becomes the spirit of life. Simply speaking, the life of God is in the Spirit of God, and the Spirit of God enters into our spirit. Thus, the three are mingled as one and become the spirit of life.

Originally our spirit was merely the spirit of man, and it was dead. Now when the Spirit of God enters, He not only enlivens our spirit but also adds the life of God into our spirit. Now not only is our spirit alive, but it also has the life of God. Moreover, it is not only the spirit; it is the spirit of life. All the consciousness of life in the spirit enables us to know this spirit. When we walk by setting the mind on the spirit, and when our actions and deeds are according to this spirit, the life in this spirit causes us to have the consciousness of this life. Since this life is of God and is therefore fresh and lively, strong with power, bright and holy, real and not empty, the sense of this life makes us sense the presence of God. Thus, we feel fresh and lively, strong with power, bright and holy, real and not empty. When we have such feelings, we know we are setting our mind on the spirit, walking according to the spirit, and living in the spirit. Such feelings are the sense of life in our spirit, or the consciousness of our spirit of life, leading us from within to walk according to the spirit and live by the spirit. When we touch such feelings, we touch the spirit, and when we heed such feelings, we heed the spirit. The spirit itself is relatively difficult for us to sense, but we can easily sense such feelings of life in the spirit. If we follow such feelings closely, we can then know the spirit and live in the spirit. The life of God in our spirit can be said to be God Himself. Therefore, the sense of this life surely will make us sense God Himself. If we live in the spirit and walk by setting our mind on the spirit, the sense of this life will cause us to feel that we are in touch with God and that God is in us as our life, our power, and our all. Thus, we will be happy, restful, comfortable, and satisfied. When we thus touch God in the inner sense of life, we touch life. Thereby we know we are living in the spirit and setting our mind on the spirit.

Since the spirit, in which rests the life of the spirit of life, is the mingling of God's Spirit with our spirit, then whatever this sense of life causes us to feel must be the "story" of the Spirit of God in our spirit. The Spirit of God in our spirit reveals Christ to us, imparts God in Christ to us, and causes us to experience Christ and touch God in the spirit. Thus, it causes us to experience Christ—that is, to experience God—as our life. This also means that it causes us to experience life, that is, to experience the life of God in our spirit. When we thus experience this life, it causes us to feel the satisfaction of life, the power of life, the brightness of life, the freshness of life, and the liveliness and transcendence of life. When we have such a sense of life within us, we know we are living in the spirit and touching the spirit.

THE SENSE OF THE LAW OF THE SPIRIT OF LIFE

In the spirit of life within us, there is not only the life of God but also a law. This law is the law of the life of God. Every life has its law and is also a law in itself. The life in our body has its law within our body and is also a law in itself within our body. The law of this life, or we may say this life itself as the law, approves and accepts whatever agrees with the nature of this life. Anything which is otherwise, this law or this life as the law opposes and refuses. Likewise, the life of God in our spirit also has its law, and it is also a law in our spirit. It is of the Spirit and rests with the Spirit; therefore, its nature is entirely and absolutely spiritual. If what we are and do agrees with the spiritual nature of God's life, the law of God's life in our spirit, or we may say God's life as the law in our spirit, approves and accepts it. Otherwise, this law or God's life as the law opposes and refuses it. All that it approves and accepts is definitely from the spirit, because only that which is from the spirit can agree with its spiritual nature. Therefore, all that we are and do must be from the spirit and in the spirit. Then the law of life in our spirit will approve and accept it.

This law of life in our spirit belongs to the order of consciousness and has its own consciousness. All that it approves and accepts or opposes and refuses is made known by what it feels and what it desires us to feel. If what we are and do is in the spirit and is in agreement with the nature of the spirit of life in us, this law will make us feel that it approves and accepts it. Otherwise, this law will cause us to feel that it is opposing and refusing. Thus, by the sense of this law, we can know whether or not we are living in the spirit and walking by the spirit. Since this law is the law of the spirit of life in us, the sense of this law is the sense of the spirit of life in us. Therefore, the sense of this law can cause us to know the spirit within.

Law is a natural thing; therefore, the sense it gives us is also natural. For example, when we drink a glass of fruit juice, we naturally feel that it is sweet. This is because there is a law of the physical life in our body which naturally causes us to feel this. As soon as our lips touch the juice, we immediately taste the sweetness. This natural sense is the law of life of our body. This law naturally causes us to taste the flavor of the juice. The law of life in our spirit is also like this. We do not need others to tell us whether what we are and do as Christians is in the spirit or whether we are mindful of the spirit and pleasing to God. The law of life in our spirit naturally makes known our situation by giving us a certain sense. This natural feeling given to us by this law of life is a natural function of the spirit of life in us. By this we may easily discern whether or not we ourselves are living in the spirit.

The sense that this law of life gives us is natural; not only so, it also causes us to feel natural. The more we live in the spirit and the more what we are and do agrees with the nature of the spirit of life within us, the more this law of life in our spirit will cause us to feel natural. If we as Christians are not natural, it proves we have some problem and that we are not living in the spirit. Since the spirit of life in us is a natural law of the spirit, only when our life and work agree with its spiritual nature can we feel natural within. When we feel natural within, it proves we are living in accordance with the law of life in our spirit. This natural feeling given to us by this law of life in us causes us to know we are living in the spirit and walking according to the spirit. Thus, if we follow the law of life in our spirit, or if we follow the natural consciousness given to us by this law of life, it means we are following the spirit of life within us. To put it simply, following the sense of the law of life in our spirit is following the spirit, because the sense of the law of life in the spirit is the sense of the spirit itself.

THE SENSE OF PEACE

The spirit of life in us is not only the place where the Spirit of God and the life of God dwell, it is also the place where the new man is. Furthermore, the spirit in us—the spirit mingled with the life of God—is also the new man within us. If in our outward action and behavior we mind the spirit of life within us, then we are living by the spiritual new man within us. In this way our inner man and our outward actions are in agreement, hence, natural and peaceful. We can say that this consciousness of being natural and peaceful is the result produced by the sense of the law of the spirit of life. If we mind the spirit of life within us, we will naturally walk and live according to the law of the spirit of life within us. This will cause us to feel natural within and have the sense of peace. This sense of peace and the sense of life go hand in hand. The sense of life is fresh and lively; the sense of peace is natural and at ease. The sense of life is satisfaction and fullness of vigor; the sense of peace is rest and comfort. If we mind the spirit and walk and live by the spirit, we will not only have the sense of life, feeling fresh, lively, satisfied, and vigorous, but also have the sense of peace, feeling natural, at ease, restful, and comfortable. Such a sense is also the sense of the spirit. Once we have such a sense, we may know that we are living in the spirit. When we follow such a sense, we follow the sense of the spirit, which means that we follow the spirit. Such a sense enables us to know the spirit and recognize the spirit. The more we walk according to the spirit and live in the spirit, the richer and deeper this kind of sense within us will become.

THE SENSE OF DEATH

There is a contrast in Romans 8:6. The apostle says that the result of setting the mind on the flesh is death, and the result of setting the mind on the spirit is life and peace. This word reveals that just as the flesh is versus the spirit, so also the result of setting the mind on the flesh, which is death, is opposite to the results of setting the mind on the spirit, which are life and peace. Thus, the apostle tells us here that death is not only the opposite of life but also the opposite of peace. Therefore, the sense of death is not only the opposite of the sense of life but also the opposite of the sense of peace. The sense of life makes us feel fresh, lively, satisfied, and vigorous; the sense of death makes us feel the opposite of these—old, deadened, empty, and powerless. The sense of peace makes us feel natural, at ease, restful, and comfortable. The consciousness of death makes us feel just the opposite of these—unnatural, uneasy, unrestful, and uncomfortable. Thus, whenever we feel inwardly deadened, depressed, empty, dry, weak and powerless, dark and dull, or unrestful, uneasy, uncomfortable, out of harmony, full of conflict, unnatural, sad, and bound, we should know we are not living in the spirit; rather, we are living in the opposite of the spirit, which is the flesh.

The flesh the apostle speaks of here refers not only to the lusts of our flesh but also to our entire old man. All that belongs to our inward new man belongs to the spirit; likewise, all that belongs to our outward old man belongs to the flesh. Whatever is not from the spirit and does not belong to the spirit is from the flesh and belongs to the flesh. The soul differs from the flesh, yet because the soul has already fallen and become captive to the flesh, all that is from the soul or belongs to the soul is also from the flesh and belongs to the flesh. Thus, if we live by the soul, we live by the flesh. Whether we set the mind on the flesh or set the mind on the soul, we are in both cases setting the mind on the flesh. The result of setting the mind on the flesh is death. This sense of death causes us to feel either depressed and empty or unrestful and uneasy. Whenever we have such consciousness, we should know that we are mindful of the flesh and that we are living either in the flesh or in the soul. Such a sense causes us to know the opposite of the spirit, which is the flesh, and to recognize it. Thus, by knowing the opposite of the spirit, we may know the spirit itself.

Whatever we do, regardless of whether we think it is right or wrong, spiritual or unspiritual, if deep within us we feel restless, uneasy, empty, and depressed, it proves that we are walking by the flesh and not living in the spirit. Even in praying and preaching, not to mention doing other things, including things which are not good, if we feel empty and depressed within, dissatisfied or unhappy, then it is proof that we are praying or preaching by the flesh, not in the spirit. Many times, by our mind or by the flesh (because it is not in the spirit), we pray as if we are reciting from a book. The more we pray, the more we feel dry and depressed, without watering and joy. After praying, we only feel empty; we do not feel satisfied. Such prayer by our mind makes our spirit incapable of obtaining the supply of life. Instead, it only touches the sense of death. Although what we prayed may have been quite appropriate, it was not in the spirit. Therefore, we could not touch the watering and joy of life and peace, but sensed only the dryness and depression of death. Many times, our preaching is also like this. When we preach not according to the spirit but by our mind, we feel empty and dry within, and we sense death. We do not feel satisfied or watered, and we do not have the sense of life. If we were in the spirit, and if we spoke by the spirit, we would feel satisfied and restful within, which means we would sense life and peace. Thus, by such a sense we can know whether what we do is in the flesh or in the spirit. Such a sense can cause us to know the flesh, and by knowing the flesh to know the spirit.

Death not only causes us to have such depressed, empty, uneasy, and unhappy feelings but also makes us lose the sense of life. Such feelings of death are warnings to us, urging us to be delivered from the flesh and live in the spirit. If we have such a sense of death, yet we continue to live in the flesh and act and behave by the flesh, after a continued period of time, death can cause our spirit within to lose consciousness and become numb. If our spirit within is numb and unconscious, it is because we have lived by the flesh for such an extended period that our spirit is damaged by death. Thus, we can and we should know how we are treating our spirit and whether or not we are living in the spirit.

KNOWING THE SPIRIT BY THE SENSE OF THE SPIRIT

All the senses of which we have spoken are those which the spirit of life within us causes us to have. Therefore, we may say that they are the senses of the spirit. If we want to know the spirit directly, it is somewhat difficult, but it is comparatively easy to know the spirit itself by such senses of the spirit. We cannot quite apprehend directly what the spirit actually is, but by the sense of the spirit, it is not difficult for us to know it. If we walk and live by closely following the sense of the spirit, then we are following the spirit and setting our mind on the spirit. If we follow the naturalness of the law of the Spirit of life, take care of the sense of life and peace, heed the warning given to us by the sense of death, and live in these senses, then we are living in the spirit. These senses are from the spirit; therefore, they can cause us to touch the spirit and thereby know the spirit.

CHAPTER FIVE

DISCERNING THE SOUL FROM THE SPIRIT

Scripture Reading: 1 Thes. 5:23; Heb. 4:12; 1 Cor. 2:14

We have seen that by the sense of the spirit we can know the spirit. Now we will see the difference between the soul and the spirit. If we can discern the difference between the soul and the spirit, we then can deny the soul and be delivered from the soul in all matters of our living and service in order to live before God by the spirit and serve God by the spirit.

THE DIFFERENCE
BETWEEN THE SOUL AND THE SPIRIT

Ordinarily, people confuse the soul and the spirit, thinking they are the same thing. The so-called psychologists analyze man and divide him into two parts: the metaphysical and the physical. The physical part refers to the body, and the metaphysical refers to the psyche, which is the soul spoken of in the Bible. They say that within the body of man there is only the psyche, the soul. However, the Bible tells us that within man, besides the soul, there is the spirit. First Thessalonians 5:23 does not speak only of the "soul" but "spirit and soul." The spirit and the soul are two things and are different. Thus, Hebrews 4:12 speaks of the dividing of soul and spirit.

If we desire to have true spiritual growth in life and proper spiritual knowledge in service, we must know that the spirit and the soul are two different things, and we must be able to differentiate the soul from the spirit, discerning what is the soul and what is the spirit, what is soulish and what is spiritual.

SOUL VERSUS SPIRIT

First Corinthians 2:14-15 speaks of two classes of men. One is the soulish man, and the other is the spiritual man. This shows us that man can live by and belong to either of these two different things, the soul or the spirit. Man can either live by the soul and belong to the soul, thereby becoming a soulish man, or he can live by the spirit and belong to the spirit, thereby becoming a spiritual man. If a man is spiritual, he can then discern the things of the Spirit of God. If, however, he is soulish, he cannot receive such things, and he cannot even know them. This makes it clear that the soul is in contrast to the spirit. The spirit can communicate with God and discern the things of the Spirit of God. The soul, however, cannot handle or understand the things of the Spirit of God. The spirit delights in appreciating and receiving the things of God, but the soul does not. Not only does it not receive such things, but it considers them foolish.

In the Bible not only is there Romans 8, which shows us that the flesh is opposed to the spirit, but there is also 1 Corinthians 2, which shows us that the soul also is opposed to the spirit. When a man lives by the flesh, he is of the flesh and not of the spirit. Likewise, when a man lives by the soul, he is of the soul and not of the spirit. When speaking of the flesh, Romans 8 emphasizes its relationship to sin; therefore, all who sin are fleshly. However, the soul is not necessarily directly related to sin. Many times man may not sin and is not fleshly, as man sees it, yet still he is soulish and not spiritual. (Strictly speaking, when man is soulish, he is also fleshly, because the soul of man has fallen under the flesh. But when we speak of the soul itself, there is a difference between being of the soul and being of the flesh.) Thus, even if we do not sin and have been freed from sin, so that in man's eyes we are not fleshly, this does not mean that we are necessarily spiritual and not soulish. Neither does it mean that we can truly understand the things of the Spirit of God or that we can perceive, apprehend, appreciate, and receive the things of God. We often think that if we could only be freed from sin and cease from indulging the flesh, we could then be spiritual, communicate with God, and understand the things of the Spirit of God. No, this is not necessarily so. It is quite possible that, though we seem to have been freed from sin and have ceased from indulging the flesh, we still live by the soul and not by the spirit.

The salvation of the Lord delivers us not only from sin and the flesh but also from the soul. The purpose of the Lord's salvation is not only that we should not be in sin and in the flesh but also that we should not be in the soul but in the spirit. His salvation would save us not only to the degree of morality that we become a moral man, but even more to the degree of spirituality so that we become a spiritual man. It is quite possible that a man of good morals is a soulish man, a man who lives by the soul. Thus, a brother or sister may be very moral and very good, yet as to the spiritual things of God he or she may not be enlightened, may not desire or appreciate them, and even may not receive them, because he or she is living by the soul and is soulish.

THE IMPOTENCE OF THE SOUL
IN SPIRITUAL THINGS

First Corinthians 2:14 says, "But a soulish man does not receive the things of the Spirit of God...and he is not able to know them." This word speaks clearly and thoroughly concerning the condition of the soul as to the things of the Spirit of God. The soul "does not receive" the things of the Spirit of God and "is not able to know them." The soul does not desire the things of the Spirit of God, nor can it receive them. Even if it wants to, it cannot, because it is not able to know or understand them. The nature of the soul is not in accord with the things of the Spirit of God. Therefore, it neither wants nor receives the things of God. Moreover, it also has no ability to know the things of God. Therefore, as to the things of the Spirit of God, a man living by the soul has no feeling, no interest, and no desire; neither does he seek them, receive them, or even understand them. For this reason God must deliver us from the soul so that we do not live by the soul. Then He can make us love, understand, and receive the things of His Spirit.

We must be clear concerning the impotence of the soul in spiritual things and regard it as an important matter. The soul does not receive the things of the Spirit of God and neither can it know them. A brother or sister who lives by the soul can be very good, well-behaved, and virtuous, but he or she definitely cannot know spiritual things and may not even thirst for spiritual things. I have met many such brothers and sisters. They are very careful in their conduct, and their behavior may be said to be faultless, yet they cannot understand spiritual things, and they do not seek them. They evaluate themselves and others by the standard of human morality, good and evil, right or wrong, and in all matters they are short of the consciousness and insight of the Spirit of God. It may be that they are clear in their mind and strong in their intellect, but they are not enlightened in their spirit, and the consciousness of their spirit is insensitive. You may call them *good* Christians, but you cannot call them *spiritual* Christians. As far as their conduct is concerned, they are really good. They know how to behave and how to handle things; they are intelligent and alert, diligent and thorough. But as soon as they touch the things of the Spirit of God, they are lost. It is as if they were wood or stone, with no consciousness or understanding faculty at all. Moreover, toward spiritual things they are often cold in heart; they are not only slow in understanding but also slothful in seeking.

Hence, good Christians are not necessarily spiritual Christians. Spiritual Christians are not merely good in their behavior; they live in the spirit, having the sense of the spirit, understanding spiritual things, knowing the ways of God from within, and having proficiency in spiritual things. Goodness and spirituality are very different. Many brothers and sisters are good, but they are not spiritual; they are good, but they do not live in the spirit. You touch goodness in them, but you do not touch the spirit. You see the virtues of man in them, but you do not smell the savor of God. From a certain standpoint they do not seem to be fleshly, yet they definitely are soulish. Though they do not give rein to the flesh, they also do not live in the spirit. Though they do not live in sin, yet they live in themselves. Though they do not approve of sinful things, they also do not thirst after spiritual things. Though they do not sin according to the flesh, they live by the self, which is the soul. The soul is the source of their life and the medium of their living. They are soulish people, living in the soul and by the soul. Therefore, they do not desire spiritual things, neither can they understand them.

THE CONTENT OF THE SOUL

The soul is our personality, our ego; therefore, the soul is our self. That which is included in our soul, analytically speaking, is the mind, the emotion, and the will—these three parts. The mind is the organ of man's thinking. It is what we usually speak of as the brain. (Physiologically it is the brain, and psychologically it is the mind.) It is the major part of the soul. Man's thinking, meditating, considering, and remembering are all functions of the mind in the soul. Man after the fall, especially today's man, lives largely in the mind and is directed by the thoughts of the mind. As man thinks, so man behaves. Man's action is always tied to man's thought. There is hardly one person who does not live according to his thought. Thus, regardless of who or what we are considering, we must begin with man's thought in order to win man's mind. Nowadays there are so many theories, schools, and educational methods, and they all have one aim: dealing with man's thought to win man's mind. If you can win a man's mind by his thought, you can then gain him, because man lives in the mind, which is the intellect, and is directed by the thought of the mind.

The emotion in the soul is the organ of man's love, anger, sorrow, and joy. Man loves, detests, rejoices, mourns, and is excited or depressed—these are all functions of the emotion in man's soul. There are many who are emotional. They are rich in emotion and very easily stirred. They often deal with matters by their emotion. With such people, when you reason with them in thought, it is often difficult to get through, but you can very easily move their emotion.

The will in the soul is the organ of man's decision making. Man decides, determines, judges, chooses, receives, and refuses—these are all functions of the will in man's soul.

Some people are in the mind, some are in the emotion, and there are some who are in the will. Just as those who are in the mind or emotion live in their mind or emotion, so those who are in the will likewise live in their will. As the mind or emotion respectively is the strongest part of those who are in them, so is the will. One who is in the will is strong in his decision and determination. Once he has determined upon some course of action, you have no way to change him. You may reason with him, but he does not care for reason. You may appeal to him with emotion, but he has no regard for emotion. He is one who acts by his will and is in the will.

The soul is comprised of these three parts—mind, emotion, and will. These three parts are simultaneously present in everyone. Everyone has a mind, emotion, and will. However, some are more in the mind, some are rich in emotion, and others are strong in the will.

Some are very clear in their thinking and very quick in their mind. Whenever something comes up, they think carefully before acting. If they have not thought things through, no matter how you try to move them with emotion, it is impossible. If you want to win them, you must use reason. They are living in the mind, or the intellect; they are the intellectual ones.

Some especially abound in emotion. It seems as if they do not have a mind and do not think, but have only emotion. Such people often make a mess of things by their emotion. If you reason with them, they frequently neither care nor understand and are not moved in their heart. If you deal with them with emotion, it is very easy to touch their inward part. A thousand or ten thousand reasons are not as powerful toward them as one or two tears. Sometimes, no matter how you reason with them, you cannot win them over, but if you shed a few tears, you can win them over. They only care for emotion, not for reason. This is because they are not in the intellect, but in the emotion.

Some people's will is especially strong. In everything they have some proposal or idea. And once they make a decision, they are very firm and cannot be easily changed. Such people usually are quite stable and stubborn, caring neither for emotion nor for reason. They decide and plan everything by their obstinate will. They set forth ideas and establish policies. You reason with them, but they do not understand. You use emotion with them, but they are not moved. They are neither in the intellect nor in the emotion, but in the will.

THE SOULISH MAN

Regardless of whether a man is in the mind, in the emotion, or in the will, he is soulish. Regardless of whether a man lives in the mind, in the emotion, or in the will, he lives in the soul. Regardless of whether a man lives by the mind, by the emotion, or by the will, he lives by the soul. Therefore, it is very easy for us to judge whether a man is soulish. We only need to see whether or not he acts by the mind, emotion, or will, and whether or not he lives in the mind, emotion, or will. As long as he acts and behaves by any one of these three, or as long as he lives in any one of these three, he is a soulish man.

A soulish man often is what is called "a good man." He is frequently faultless in man's eyes. Clear thinking always brings the praise of men to those who act by it. Moderate emotion always brings the approval of men to those who live in it. A firm will also often brings the commendation of men to those who rely on it. But when a man lives in these, though he is not living in sin, he is also not living in the spirit. Though before men he seems to be without sin and faultless, before God his spirit is blocked, and his spiritual understanding is dull.

Once in a certain place I met a co-worker. His conduct was very good, but he lived too much in the mind, or in the intellect; therefore, it was difficult for him to understand or comprehend spiritual things. Whenever I spoke to him concerning matters of serving God, I was quite fearful that his eyes would roll. When I spoke, he would listen until he almost got the point, and then his eyes would roll, and he became confused again. When his eyeballs were rolling, it meant that his mind was considering. He only used his mind to consider; he did not use his spirit to sense the things of God. Therefore, it was exceedingly difficult for him to understand and sense spiritual things.

Thinking is frequently the difficulty and hindrance of the brothers in spiritual things. Many brothers often use thinking to deal with spiritual things, and they use their intellect to touch the matters of the service. They think they can understand spiritual things by exercising their mind. They do not know that the mind, being part of the soul, cannot understand the spirit. A man living in the mind lives in the soul and definitely becomes a soulish man with no ability to understand spiritual things.

Just as the mind is the difficulty of the brothers in spiritual things, so the emotion is frequently the hindrance of the sisters. The reason many sisters cannot understand or sense spiritual things is that they are too much in the emotion. In the churches in various places, I have seen many good sisters who have enthusiasm and love, who are careful in their behavior, and whose conduct is sober; yet when it comes to spiritual things, they lack consciousness, and they can hardly apprehend them. This is because they live too much in their emotion and act too much by their emotion. Apparently, emotion is not sin, but emotion prevents them from living in the spirit, from touching the things of God by their spirit, from having any spiritual sense, and from understanding spiritual things. Emotion is their pitfall; it keeps them in the sphere of the soul, living by the soul and being a soulish person.

For many brothers, the will is also a difficulty and hindrance to their understanding the spiritual things. Even some sisters have this problem. They judge and decide on matters too much by their will, so unknowingly they live in the soul, having no spiritual sense or understanding in spiritual things.

Whichever part of the soul a person is in, he very easily acts by that part and lives in that part. Whenever one who is in the mind encounters anything, he naturally thinks through the matter again and again, considering it from many angles. One who is in the emotion unconsciously cares very much for the emotion in dealing with others and handling things. A person with a strong will very easily leans on his will in dealing with people and matters. Whichever part of the soul a person lives in easily and naturally, he definitely belongs to that part. If you see a person who very naturally thinks, considers, weighs, and measures every matter, you can be sure he must be one who acts by the intellect; therefore, he is one who is in the mind. If a person is easily stirred when facing things, smiling and weeping quickly, happy for one moment and depressed the next, you know that he must be one who abounds in emotion and is emotional. If, whenever you encounter things, you plan and decide without any effort, and your will comes out to deal and function without any special exercise on your part, then undoubtedly you are one who is strong in will and who is in the will. Whichever part of the soul is strong or abounds in a person, it is always that part which is in the forefront whenever he encounters anything and deals with it. Whichever part of a person's soul takes the lead in dealing with things, it is a proof that he is in that particular part, and it is also a proof that he is a soulish man.

THE SPIRITUAL MAN

If we can recognize what kind of person is soulish, it is not difficult to realize what kind of person is spiritual. Since a soulish person lives by the mind, emotion, or will, a spiritual person must be one who does not live by these. Since a soulish person lives by the soul and not by the spirit, then a spiritual person must live in the spirit and not in the soul. Although spiritual persons also have souls, and although the mind, emotion, or will in their soul may even be stronger and abound more than that of ordinary soulish persons, yet they do not live by these soulish organs, nor do they live in them. They live by the spirit and in the spirit, and they allow the spirit to be the master and source of their action and behavior. The spirit in them occupies the preeminent position; it is the source of their behavior and starting point of their action. The soul in them is in the position of submission. Although the mind, emotion, and will in their souls also function, these are all subjected under the ruling of the spirit and are directed by the spirit. Although they use their mind, emotion, or will, they always follow the sense of the spirit in using these organs of the soul. They are not like soulish persons, who let the soul be the master in everything, who allow the mind, emotion, or will of the soul to stand in the forefront to lead and to function. They deny the preeminence of the soul and refuse the leading of the mind, emotion, or will. Thus, they allow the spirit to be the master in them. They allow the spirit to direct their whole being so that they may follow the sense of the spirit. Whenever they encounter something, they do not first use the mind, emotion, or will of the soul to contact and deal with it. Rather, they use their spirit first to touch and to sense it, seeking first in the spirit for the Lord's feeling as to this matter. After they have touched the Lord's feeling in their spirit, they use the mind in the soul to understand the sense in the spirit, the emotion in the soul to express it, and the will in the soul to carry it out. Although they use the organs of the soul, they are not soulish, and they do not live by the life of the soul. They are spiritual, living by the life of the spirit, and the soul is simply an organ for them to employ.

AN ABNORMAL CONDITION

We have seen that a fallen man, dead as he is in spirit, can only live by the soul. But we who are saved and have an enlivened spirit can live by the spirit. Furthermore, God saves us so that we can return to the spirit and live by the spirit. The fall of man caused man to fall from the spirit to the soul so that man no longer lives by the spirit but by the soul. God's salvation saves man from the soul to the spirit so that man does not live by the soul but by the spirit. However, many who are saved still do not live this way. Some remain in the soul and live by the soul because they do not know the difference between the spirit and the soul and the matters involved therein. Moreover, they do not know that God's desire is that they be delivered from the soul and live in the spirit. There are some who know that their spirit has been enlivened, that it is different from their soul, and that God wants them to live in their spirit; nevertheless, they continue to remain in the soul and live by the soul. This is because they are accustomed to living by the soul and not by the spirit and because they do not consider living in the spirit important. These Christians, who do not know the difference between the spirit and the soul and do not know that God wants us to be delivered from the soul and live in the spirit, think that to live by the mind, emotion, or will of the soul is fitting and necessary. They also think that if only they are careful and faultless, they are all right. However, they do not know that as far as Christians are concerned, this is far too poor!

God does not intend to deliver us merely from faults to a state of faultlessness. He intends to deliver us even more from the soul to the spirit. He wants us not only to live a faultless life, but even more to live a spiritual life, a spiritually fault-less life. He wants us to live a faultless life not by the soul but by the spirit. Yet because of their ignorance, many Christians still live by the soul, and they strive and struggle to be those that are faultless by their soul-life. Although their spirit has already been enlivened, they do not know they should use their spirit and live by their spirit. They want to make them-selves perfect men, living a satisfactory life by the power of the soul alone. Their view and judgment of things and their love and inclination are all in the soul, not in the spirit. Although they are well-behaved Christians, and their conduct and behavior are blameless, they still are living in the soul, not in the spirit. It may be granted that their thoughts are clean, their emotions are balanced, and their decisions are accurate, but they are still soulish, not spiritual. Their condition as far as Christians are concerned is abnormal. They are living the abnormal Christian life. Even if they are successful, they can only satisfy themselves. Sometimes some are truly satisfied with their success, a success which is truly doubtful. However, they cannot please God, for God wants man to be delivered from the soul and live by the spirit.

There are Christians who have some knowledge of the difference between the spirit and the soul and of God's desire for us to be delivered from the soul and live in the spirit, yet they are still living by the soul. They are also living an abnormal Christian life. Although they know that their spirit has already been enlivened, they do not live by it. Although they know that God wants them to be delivered from the soul and live in the spirit, they still remain in the soul and live by the soul. Although they know that man should contact God in the spirit, they still use the soul to touch the things of God. They know they have a spirit, yet they do not use their spirit. They know they should live by the spirit, yet they do not live in the spirit. They find it convenient to use the mind, emotion, or will of the soul and are not accustomed to using the spirit. Hence, they neglect living by the spirit. Whenever anything happens, they always firstly use their mind, emotion, or will to deal with it. They do not firstly use their spirit to contact it. At most they can only be good and faultless Christians, although this is really doubtful. However, they cannot be spiritual Christians. They can only satisfy themselves; they cannot please God. They can only be commended by men; they cannot receive the praise of God. They still need the deliverance of God—not deliverance from sin but deliverance from the soul and not deliverance from the filthy flesh condemned by men but deliverance from the clean soul commended by men. Otherwise, they are still strangers and outsiders to the things of the Spirit of God.

THE WAY OF DELIVERANCE
FROM THE SOUL

How can we be delivered from the soul? This requires revelation from two standpoints, one concerning the soul and the other concerning the cross. We must see that the soul is impotent in the things of God and worthless in spiritual things. No matter how excellent and strong any part of our soul may be, it still cannot apprehend the things of God or understand spiritual things. However clean our mind, however balanced our emotion, and however proper our will, these can never make us spiritual. We must also see that our soul and all things that belong to it have already been crucified on the cross of Christ. In Galatians 2:20, when the apostle says, "I am crucified with Christ," the "I" he refers to is the soul. The soul, in God's estimation, deserves only death. Moreover, our soul has already been taken care of by God through the cross of Christ. Hence, we should not value the things of our soul. Rather, we should only admit that our soul should die, that it deserves death, and that it is already dead. Such revelation and vision enable us to condemn the soul, deny the soul, reject the soul, forbid the soul to take the lead in all things, and in everything give no ground to the soul. By the Spirit we put the soul to death; we allow the Spirit to put to death the soul-life and to deal with the activity of the soul by the cross.

We must see how powerless the soul is before God, how it cannot comprehend the things of God and cannot please God. We must also see God's estimation of the soul and how He deals with our soul. Only then can we deny the soul, reject the soul, and be delivered from the soul. Therefore, we must ask the Lord to make us see not only the impotence of the soul but also the dealing of the cross with the soul. Thus, in everything we will learn to reject the soul and not live by the soul. One who is in the mind should refuse his intellect in all spiritual things; he should put aside completely such functions as thinking and considering and return to the spirit, using the spirit to sense the consciousness of God. When he reads the Bible, prays, or speaks about spiritual things, he should refuse his thinking, imagining, theorizing, and investigating, and follow closely the sense in his spirit and move on in the fellowship of God. One who abounds in emotion should refuse his emotion in everything. He should not allow his emotion to lead and direct, but let the Spirit deal with his emotion. Thus, he can sense the will of God in the spirit. He should fear his emotion just as he fears sin, and in fear and trembling live in the spirit, not being directed or influenced by his emotion. One who is in the will should see his will as the enemy of God in the things of God, as the opponent of the spirit. Thus, he will condemn, refuse, and deny his will. He should allow the Holy Spirit to break his will by the cross so that he does not live before God by his firm and strong will but by the consciousness in his spirit.

Whichever part of the soul we are in, we should condemn and refuse it. Whether it is our mind, emotion, or will, they all should be broken and dealt with. In all the things of God, we should refuse the leading of the mind, emotion, and will. Rather, we should let the spirit occupy the first place to govern, direct, and employ our mind, emotion, and will. In this way we can be delivered from the soul. Then, on the one hand, we can employ all the organs in the soul by our spirit, and on the other hand, we will not live by the soul. Hence, we will not be soulish but spiritual.

CHAPTER SIX

THE SERVICE WHICH IS IN SPIRIT

Scripture Reading: 2 Cor. 4:7, 10, 16; 3:5-6

NOT LIVING BY THE SOUL

In the previous chapter we saw the distinction between the soul and the spirit. We also saw that a saved person should live before God by the spirit and not by the soul. As we said before, the soul is just the self. Those who live in the soul are living in the self. We further saw that the soul has three main parts: the mind, emotion, and will. One who lives in any of these three parts is living in the soul and in the self. One who lives in the mind is just living in the self. One who lives in the emotion is also living in the self. Furthermore, one who lives in the will is living in the self. Living in the self is living in the soul, that is, living by the soul. Even if one's behavior is perfect and one's living is blameless, what is lived out is still the self and not God. It is not the issue of God's operation from within him. Rather, it is the living out of his own mind, emotion, and will. Therefore, a saved person should not live this way.

THE PURPOSE OF GOD'S SALVATION

I believe, brothers and sisters, you are clear that the purpose of God's salvation is not merely to save us from sin but even more to save us from our self, from our soul. God does not want us only to live a life of goodness and be a good man. Rather, He wants us to live the life of God and be a God-man, a regenerated man. We should not live in our mind, emotion, or will. Perhaps our mind is sound, our emotion is clean, and our will is not crooked, but they are still the elements of the self. If we live in them, we live in the self. Perhaps they are good, but they are not God living out from within us. Therefore, we must reject them and hate the living that is lived out by them. We must always remember that in His salvation God wants to save us to such an extent that He becomes our life and our living so that we can live by Him and in Him, thereby living Him out. He is in us as our life, and He lives out from within us as our living. He is within us through the indwelling of His Spirit in our spirit. His Spirit and our spirit are mingled together and have become one spirit. Only when we live in this spirit are we living in Him. If we live in the soul, we are living in the self. No matter whether we live in the mind, in the emotion, or in the will, we are not living in the spirit and therefore not living in God. Consequently, what we live out may be very good, but it is either of our mind, our emotion, or our will; it is absolutely not God living out from within us. There are two sources: the spirit and the soul. God is in the spirit, and we are in the soul. If we live in the spirit, God will have the ground in us. If we live in the soul, we ourselves will have the ground in us. If we live in the soul, we will express ourselves. If we live in the spirit, we will express God. These two different sources have two different expressions. One is the spirit, and the other is the soul. One is God, and the other is the self. God is in the spirit, and the self is in the soul. If we live in the spirit, we live out God. If we live in the soul, we live out the self. We must be very clear about these two sources and their two expressions.

THE OUTER MAN AND THE INNER MAN

The Bible tells us that our soul is our outer man with the mind, emotion, and will. Our spirit, however, is our inner man. Our soul, which is our outer man, has the life of Adam and belongs to the old creation. Our spirit, which is our inner man, has the life of Christ and belongs to the new creation. Our outer man is our natural soul, whereas our inner man is our regenerated spirit. The life of our outer man is the life of man. The life of our inner man is the life of God. Every saved person may be considered a double person in that each one has an outer man and an inner man with an outer life and an inner life. A true Christian certainly is a double person consisting of the outer man and the inner man. The outer man is his self; the inner man is God indwelling him. The outer man has the human life, whereas the inner man has the divine life.

TWO POSSIBILITIES OF LIVING

Thus, a Christian has two possibilities of living. One possibility is to live in the outer man and the other possibility is to live in the inner man. Every Christian must bear the responsibility for either living in the outer man or living in the inner man. As we have said before, this is like having two kinds of lamps in your room; one is an oil lamp and the other is an electric lamp. It is up to you if you want to light the oil lamp or switch on the electric lamp. We have two lives and can live out two kinds of living as two kinds of people. Do we want to live by our human life or by the divine life? Do we want to live in the outer man or in the inner man? It is entirely up to us.

SERVING BY THE SOUL BEING OF THE SELF

Since we should not live by the soul, we should also not serve by the soul. The apostle says that we are not sufficient of ourselves for the ministry, but that our sufficiency is from God (2 Cor. 3:5-6). To be by the self is to be by the soul. We do not serve as ministers by our soul. As ministers of the new covenant, we serve under the new covenant by the spirit, not by the soul. However, we often think that all we need is to serve and that we do not need to care by what we serve. We often think that as long as our service is right and good, we do not need to worry about anything else because everything is fine without any problems. This is not true! Even a proper or good service may still have a problem. Indeed, many services that are right and good have a problem. For example, a brother may be rich in his emotion and truly care for the brothers. One day he suddenly remembers two brothers who often miss the meetings, so he decides to visit them and eventually he goes. I would ask you, is it good for him to visit the brothers like this? Some may say it is not good, but how can you say this? It is not good to go watch a movie or to sin and do evil, but is it also not good to visit the brothers? You cannot say that. It is really good. It is not evil but good. It appears to be a good thing done for the Lord. We have to ask, though, did the brother whom I just mentioned visit the brothers from his soul or from his spirit? Did the Spirit of God send him, or did he go on his own? Some would say he went from his soul. Yes, he went from his soul, not from his spirit. He himself wanted to go; it was not the Spirit of God sending him.

We must ask further. Out of which part of the soul did he go? Some may say he went out of the emotion, others out of the will, and still others out of the mind. These three answers cover all three parts of the soul. Actually, he acted from all three parts. His visiting was initiated in his emotion, passed through his mind, and was decided by the will; therefore, it was entirely out of the soul. Whatever comes out of the urge of the emotion, the consideration of the mind, and the decision of the will is from the soul.

We must also ask whether such a visiting from the soul is carried out through the outer man or the inner man. Naturally, it is through the outer man. Moreover, we must ask whether it is done out of the self or out of God. Naturally, it is out of the self.

Since this going is done out of the self, it is also of the self. Then, is the self good or bad? Some may say it is not good; they are absolutely right. The self is bad. Everyone's self is bad. Yet it is marvelous that now a good thing can come out of the bad self. How can this be? How can something good be in something bad? How can a good thing come out of a bad thing? How do we explain this?

This shows that the things which we think are good can come out of the self. Whatever comes out of the self comes out of the soul. It does not matter how good they are in our eyes, the source is still the soul, the self.

Many times the things that come out of the self are very good, but the source is bad. Therefore, we must see that even the good things in the service, such as visiting the brothers, can possibly come out from the soul. This kind of service cannot be considered the service of the spirit. It can only be considered the service of the soul. This kind of service might be needed, but is it acceptable? Some brothers say that we should not accept it. But many times is our service not this kind of service? We do good things, but they come out from the wrong source. Many times when we serve, we are simply doing the right thing from the wrong source. This should not be. We should visit the brothers, but we should not visit them by our soul. We should not be sent by the soul to visit the brothers.

DOING RIGHT THINGS FROM THE RIGHT SOURCE

This kind of visitation is a right thing, yet it is from the wrong source. A right thing should come out of the right source. The matter of visiting the brothers should come out of the spirit to be proper. Both the matter and source must be right. Our problem now is that the brothers and sisters everywhere are almost all doing the right things from the wrong source. It is right to love the brothers, it is right to minister to them, it is right to visit them, and it is right to help them. All these matters are right. But what is their source? Do they come out of the spirit or the soul? Whatever comes out of the spirit is right; whatever comes out of the soul is wrong. We should not merely ask if the things we do are right or wrong. We should also ask if the source is right or wrong. Therefore, we should not only ask, What am I doing? We should more importantly ask, By what am I doing it? From what am I doing it? Am I doing this by the spirit or by the soul? Am I doing it out of the spirit or out of the soul? Oh, brothers and sisters, this question is too crucial in the matter of our service to God! Perhaps what you are doing is right, but you may be doing the right thing out of the wrong source. Therefore, we must check the source of everything we do. Is it from the spirit as the source or from the soul as the source? Whatever is done with the soul as its source should not be done, even if it is right. Whatever comes from the soul, whether it is good or bad, right or wrong, should be rejected and condemned.

CONDEMNING EVERYTHING THAT IS
FROM THE SOUL

Therefore, we must learn to condemn everything that is from the soul and everything that belongs to the soul. We must condemn the emotion, the mind, and the will, which all belong to the soul, and we must also condemn everything that comes out of them. We must realize that our emotion, mind, and will are soulish things and that whatever comes out of them are from the soul. If these things have the ground in us, it is the soul that has the ground in us. If we live in these, then we are living in the soul. If we see this, know this, and understand this, we will condemn these things, and we will not only condemn them, but we will also judge them and confess the fact that the soul has already been put to death on the cross. We will confess that our emotion, mind, and will have all been crucified. Because we have been crucified with the Lord on the cross, everything belonging to us has also been crucified with Him. Just as God put our soul to death through the cross, so also He put all the parts of our soul to death through the cross. Today before God, we also condemn, judge, and apply the Lord's death on the cross to these things. Before God we deny that these things have any ground in us. We see that these things have already been crucified, that they were hung on the cross long ago. We consider our emotion, mind, and will as having been hung on the cross long ago. We must judge and condemn all the things of our soul by applying the death of the cross, that is, by experiencing the putting to death of our soul-life through the cross. The more we have this kind of judging and condemning, the better.

THE RELEASE OF THE SPIRIT

Some may think that if we condemn and judge the things of the soul, we will no longer be able to do anything. We condemn our emotion, our mind, and our will; as soon as we think about doing something, we condemn our thinking. In this way, some think, we will become wooden persons or stone persons and will not be able to do anything. However, brothers and sisters, the marvelous point is right here. This is the difference between Christians and the unsaved. If an unsaved person were to condemn his mind, emotion, and will, then he certainly would become a "stone" person. An unsaved person only has the outer man with the outward soul-life; within him there is no life but death. If he were to condemn, judge, and reject the outer man while he is inwardly dead, then he naturally would become a "wooden" person. This is what happens with the unbelievers. But we saved ones have another man and another life within. If we reject our outer man and our outer life, then our inner man and inner life will have the ground in us. If we reject, condemn, and judge our outer man, then God will bear the responsibility and cause His Spirit to live another life out from within us. If we bury a stone in the earth, it will not grow anything; once we bury it, it is finished. If, however, we bury a seed in the earth, something will grow after just a few days. An unbeliever is like a stone that has no life within. If he rejects his outer man and puts his outer life into death, then he will be finished. But we Christians are like seeds; we have a life inside that is the Lord's life. If we reject our outer life, then our inner life will grow. If we are willing to let our outer shell be broken to pieces, then our inner man will be lived out from within.

The apostle says that within us we have a "treasure," which is the Lord's life. He also says that if we always bear about in the body the putting to death of the Lord Jesus, then the life of the Lord Jesus also will be manifested in our body. This means that if we allow the Lord's death to do a killing work in our body, the Lord's life in us will be manifested. Moreover, the apostle says that our outer man is decaying, yet our inner man is being renewed. This means that if our outer man is consumed, our inner man will be able to grow. Therefore, if we reject our outer man and put him to death, then our inner man will grow stronger.

We are double people with an outer man and an inner man. Formerly we lived in our outer man, yet now God wants us to live in our inner man. However, this is not so easy. We have been living in the outer man for such a long time that we have become accustomed to it. Naturally it will be somewhat difficult for us to make a change now and live in the inner man. Even today, most of the brothers and sisters still live in the outer man by the mind, emotion, and will. Very few live before God in the inner man by the spirit. Even though they serve God and do His work, they do it by the soul and not by the spirit, from the outer man and not from the inner man. Now God wants us to learn to turn from the outer man back to the inner man. He wants us to learn to live and serve not in the outer man but in the inner man. This is learning to live or serve not by the soul but by the spirit since the outer man is the soul and the inner man is the spirit. The secret to living in the spirit and not in the soul is to judge, condemn, reject, and deny our soul. In this way the spirit gains the ground and the opportunity within us and is spontaneously lived out from within us.

For example, if you are going to visit a brother, but you realize that it is something of your emotion, it comes out of your mind, and it is decided by your will, you must immediately judge, condemn, and reject it before God. You must hate such a thing. Perhaps you will say that if this is the case, then you will not be able to visit the brothers. But it is not so! If your visiting the brothers is of the spirit, it will not be diminished by your condemning and rejecting. If God wants you to go visiting, and if the Holy Spirit has given you a burden, then the more you reject the things of the soul, the more manifest and the heavier the burden in your spirit will be. The more you reject the things of the soul, the clearer the things in your spirit will be. After you have condemned the things of the soul and rejected the activities that are from the soul, there is still a burden and a deep sense in your spirit urging you to visit the brothers. At this time, it is the spirit sending you to visit the brother. This kind of visitation is from the spirit, not from the soul; it is spiritual, not soulish. Therefore, this kind of service is called the service in spirit.

THE SERVICE WHICH IS IN SPIRIT

For example, a brother may come to you after he has an argument with his wife at home, and he tells you the problem from beginning to end. While considering which Bible verses to use to teach him concerning the problem, you remember

Ephesians 5. So you open your Bible to this chapter and read it to him, reminding him how a husband ought to love his wife. We cannot say this kind of teaching is not good. It is truly good to use the Bible to teach others. To teach the brother in this way is really a good service. However, we have to ask, is this kind of service from the soul or from the spirit? I believe that now we could all know this is from the soul because it comes from your considering. Even though the book of Ephesians was originally written under the inspiration of the Holy Spirit, it now is something you have remembered and applied with your mind. If you truly understood what spiritual service means, then you could not help the brother in this way. You would have to condemn these things from the soul and return to your spirit. When the brother is telling you his problems, you simply return to your spirit and fellowship with God in spirit. You do not think about doctrines or the Bible; rather, you touch and contact God in spirit. Perhaps, in a marvelous way, before the brother is even half-finished speaking, your spirit touches something and feels that while the argument between him and his wife was reasonable, it was too much in the flesh. The more he speaks, the more you feel that he is full of flesh. While he is speaking, you are not using your mind to think, but your spirit is touching a fleshly person. At this time, you would definitely not speak biblical doctrines to him from your mind. Instead, you would say to him from your spirit, "Brother, even though you are right, do you not feel that you are in the flesh when you speak and argue like this? Maybe your wife is completely in the wrong, but are you not in the flesh to argue like this?" When you do this, you are not helping the brother in your soul. Instead, you are ministering to him in your spirit. This is not by considering in the soul but by sensing in the spirit. Your spirit within causes you to touch his inward condition. You are in spirit, so you can touch the things within him and can recognize his flesh that is behind his words and excuses. Thus, you can speak a few living words to him from your spirit which come from God's inspiration and not from your considering. Perhaps God wants you to say to him, "Brother, God has given you such an unreasonable wife because you are too much in your reasonings. He uses such an unreasonable wife to deal with your reasoning flesh." At such a time, the Holy Spirit often has the opportunity to do a living work. Perhaps when the brother hears you speak such a word, his eyes will fill with tears, and he will say, "I feel that I should not argue, but inwardly I am not willing to submit." Perhaps you can still say to him, "Brother, you are a person of reasoning. Your flesh is all tied up in reasoning. God wants to break your flesh, so He must break your reasoning. God knows this, so He has especially given you such a precious, unreasonable wife to deal with your reasoning every day. God has prepared this wife for you to break you of your reasoning and arguing." When you speak to him in this way, you will touch his inner man and point out his problem. If you do this, you may help him break through in this matter. Later when his wife is unreasonable, he will not argue with her but will rather praise and thank the Lord. His reasoning flesh will have gone out. Wherever the cross and the Holy Spirit are, the flesh is broken. It is really a marvelous matter that the more a person reasons, the more reasonings he has. The more reasonings he has, the more he reasons, and the more he argues, the more he has to argue about. But when He stops reasoning, his wife also stops reasoning. They both have received direct and indirect spiritual help from you.

The situation described above shows that we should not serve by our mind. Now we will go on to see that we should also not serve by our emotion. For example, a sister may be troubled by her husband at home, so she comes to see me, hoping that I could give her some help. When I hear the trouble she has had, I feel very sympathetic to her. This is my emotion being moved. This cannot help her. If my spirit is strong and in a proper condition, then I must judge my emotional reaction and condemn my sympathetic heart. I must have the sense that God has not sent me to sympathize with my brothers and sisters. Rather, He has sent me to minister His life to the spirits of my brothers and sisters so that His life can swallow up all the things of death in them. Therefore, if I am in spirit, I will judge my emotion instead of using it as a means to help that sister or serve the Lord.

Furthermore, we should not only avoid serving by our mind or by our emotion, but we should also refrain from serving by our will. Perhaps I am not rich in emotions or clear in thinking, but I have a very strong will which is as solid as a great mountain. When a brother comes to see me and speaks about his problems, neither my mind nor my emotion is moved. After the brother finishes speaking, I exhort him to be at peace and patient and not to be anxious or frightened. This kind of exhortation is not from the emotion or from the mind, yet it is from the will, so I am still not ministering to him in spirit. Regardless of whether it comes from the emotion, mind, or will, I have no way to make him touch his spirit or enable him to receive the supply in his spirit. Therefore, I cannot solve his problems of life.

We must reject the mind, emotion, and will. We must reject the soul and render help to others out of the spirit that we may give them the spiritual supply. Whether we are thoughtful, sympathetic, or calm, we are of the soul. This must be condemned and rejected.

What is the service that is in spirit? It is that whatever comes out of the soul, including the mind, the emotion, and the will, regardless of whether it is bad or good, should be condemned and rejected. Thus, we can serve in spirit, and all our services will be services which are in spirit.

THE PROBLEM TODAY
AND THE WAY OF DELIVERANCE

The problem in the church today is not due to sins. Rather, it is due to the fact that many works, even many so-called "sacred works," seem good and right but are out of the human soul and are merely of man. These works are done for the Lord, but they are from the human soul—from man's zeal, man's good intention, man's perception, and man's opinion. Apparently, they are scriptural, but their source is neither God nor the spirit; rather, their source is man and the soul. It is this kind of work in Christianity today that is a huge problem. This is because outwardly the works seem good, right, and scriptural, but there is a problem with the source. The problem is not a matter of whether the work is right or wrong, but what the source of the work is and where the work comes from. Does it come from God or man? Does it come from the spirit or the soul? The work may be good, but there is something wrong with it because its source is not God but man. Zeal is frequently the source of the works today. Ideas are also the origin of many works today. Many people serve the Lord merely in their zeal and by their own ideas. If you subtract these things from their service, their service becomes empty and it equals zero. In their service there is almost nothing of the element of the spirit. This is because their service is neither of the spirit nor through the spirit.

Today our eyes must be opened, and we must be clear inwardly. Our service to God should not come out of our zeal, our ideas, or our determination. We should judge these things and let our spirit come out strongly. We should not serve God by the things of the outward man. We should condemn our zeal, judge our ideas, and reject our vigor, thereby denying everything of our self, our soul. We must stand in the death of the cross, allowing the entire outer man to be put to death by the Holy Spirit with the cross. In this way, our spirit will gain the ground in us, and it will become strong and living. Thus, we will be able to serve in spirit. Only this kind of service can help others to touch God, minister life to them, and solve their spiritual problems. May the Lord have mercy on us that we would learn to be delivered from living in the soul to living in the spirit and from serving Him in the soul to serving Him in the spirit.

Chapter Seven

THE REJECTING AND TEARING DOWN
OF THE SOUL

Scripture Reading: 2 Cor. 4:7, 10, 16

REJECTING THE THINGS OF THE SOUL

In the previous chapter we saw how to serve in spirit and how to serve God by exercising our spirit. Therefore, we must reject our soul. We also saw that the soul is composed of three functions: the mind, the emotion, and the will. If we would reject the soul, we must reject these functions of the soul. Although they are good, we still must reject them. We should not serve God by these organs. In the service to God these organs have their positions, but they should not occupy the first place. We should allow only the spirit to have the pre-eminence in our service to God. If we serve God by the mind, emotion, or will, then our spirit will definitely be suppressed and depreciated and will not have its proper position. If these functions dominate our service to God, then our spirit will lose its position and will not be able to manifest its function.

We should never allow our service to come out of our soul. We must always judge, condemn, and reject the soul. All our services should have the spirit as their source. They should all come out from the spirit and allow the spirit to be dominant, to have authority, and to control everything. This does not mean, however, that our mind, emotion, and will are of absolutely no use in our service to God. These faculties still have their place, which is secondary and not primary. They should not take the lead; rather, they should be under the control of the spirit.

This matter, however, is somewhat difficult. Because we are too accustomed to living in the mind, emotion, and will, it is hard for us to get out of them. We are in these faculties even when we pray or read the Bible, not to mention when we are doing other things. We have lived in our mind, emotion and will too deeply and for too long, so it is not easy for us to be saved from them or to get out of them. Moreover, these items are basically man himself. Just consider this: How can a person get out of himself? This is a difficult thing! It is easier for us to get out of sins and the world because these are from outside of us. It is very difficult, however, for us to not live by the self because it is not merely inside of us, but also it is simply us. It is truly hard for us not to live by the self—the mind, emotion, and will—and to live without the self by rejecting the functions of the soul. It is relatively easy not to do the things that are evil or wrong but to do the things that are good and right. However, it is truly difficult not to do things by the self or the soul but to do things by the spirit.

We must know, though, that if we do not do things by the spirit, then what we do in our service to God does not have much weight or value. Furthermore, if we do not live by the spirit, it is difficult for us to grow in the spiritual life. This may be considered a very crucial point. Whether our service will have any value and whether our spiritual life will have any growth, all these questions depend on whether we can be delivered from the self, whether we can reject the soul, and whether we can live and serve by the spirit instead of by the soul.

THE WAY OF REJECTING

If we would reject the things of the soul, then we must clearly see before God that anything that comes out of our mind, emotion, or will is a hindrance and an enemy to the spirit. If we see this, we will condemn and reject our mind, emotion, and will. In the past we loved and appreciated these things. Perhaps you were one who has imagination, intelligence, and cleverness. Maybe you were one who is rich in emotions and can easily sympathize with and care for others. Or perhaps you were one who is strong in will and has backbone and opinions. In the past you boasted in these things and you appreciated and thought highly of them. Now, however, you realize that although these things are good, they are spiritual hindrances which prevent you from touching your spirit. If you appreciate and think highly of these things, you will not be able to learn to exercise your spirit, to really touch your spirit, or to serve God in spirit. Once you have this realization, you will hate your thinking and cleverness, your sympathy and concern for others, and your views and opinions. You will condemn all these things. In the past you considered these things to be your advantages, but now you see them as your problems. This is why you condemn them. Moreover, every time you meet with some situation, you are in fear and trembling, being afraid that your mind, emotion, or will may come out first. Therefore, in every situation, you do not dare to use these items first. Rather, you reject them.

THE RESULT OF REJECTING

Only at this time, and only under such circumstances, can you truly return to the spirit. Only then can the spirit in you have the opportunity to let you touch its feeling. Thus, you can walk by the spirit, exercise the spirit, and serve God in spirit. One who serves God in spirit must be one who hates, condemns, and judges the self and who fears the self much more than he fears sin and the world. Thus, he will be able to serve God by contacting Him, touching Him, and fellowshipping with Him in spirit.

No one can contact God with the things of the soul. Since God is Spirit, if we want to contact Him, we must use our spirit. We can contact Him and fellowship with Him only in spirit. Whenever we live in our soul, we cannot contact God; instead, we lose our fellowship with Him. When we live according to our mind, emotion, and will, then we lose God. Thus, we must hate, condemn, and reject the things of our soul. If we are willing to do this, then we can return to our spirit to contact God and touch His feeling, thereby serving Him.

THE NECESSITY OF CONTACTING GOD

Our service must be the issue of our contact with God in spirit. However, this is not the case with most of our service. For example, when we preach, sometimes we speak only from our mind and our clear thinking, without having fellowship with God in our spirit and without touching His feeling. This kind of preaching, which is from the mind of the soul, does not require us to contact God and fellowship with Him. On the contrary, in this kind of preaching we have lost our fellowship with God and have become disconnected from Him.

There is another kind of preaching, however, which comes from God as the issue of one's contact and fellowship with God. Every sentence gives people the sense of touching God. With this kind of preaching, it is a secondary matter whether the listeners are moved, but the speaker himself surely is moved, touches God, and speaks out of his fellowship with God.

With respect to these two different kinds of preaching, the first kind does not require the denial of the self, fellowship with God, hating of the self, or contact with God. It is possible that the speaker has gone for a long time without fellowshipping with God or contacting Him, yet he is able to speak a message according to his mind. This kind of preaching is similar to a worldly person's making a speech; the only difference is the topic. The worldly people cover secular topics, whereas this kind of preacher covers scriptural topics. Just as the worldly speech-making is from the mind, so also this kind of preaching is from the mind. It does not require contact or fellowship with God because the mind is sufficient.

Before God, however, this kind of preaching is more filthy than sin! The reason is that this kind of preaching belongs to death. Before God death is more filthy than sin. The Old Testament shows us that the greatest offense to God is death. Sin offends against God's ways, while death offends against God Himself. Therefore, when the Old Testament people touched death, they had to purify themselves for a long time.

Any service rendered apart from one's contact with God in spirit is dead in God's eyes and is something belonging to death; hence, in God's view it is very filthy.

The preachings and prayers according to the mind seem to be spiritual and holy. In God's eyes, however, they all belong to death and come out of death, and they also come from man, from the soul. Hence, they are very filthy and void of God's Spirit, life, or element. If we have been enlightened before the Lord, we will fear this kind of preaching and prayer more than we fear committing a gross sin. If we have the light before God, then we will fear the self doing anything of service to God more than we fear committing a sin.

Many problems of the children of God today are right here. Many services, works, preachings, and prayers have not passed through God. They are not of God, from God, or the result of the fellowship and contact with God. Moreover, it seems there is no need for them to pass through God or contact God. Rather, human cleverness, human thinking, human decisiveness, human perseverance, and human zeal are sufficient for man to do these works. Man does not need to contact God, fellowship with God, or depend on God in doing these works but is fully able to declare his independence from God. These works, however, are of the soul, of man, of man's self, and in God's eyes they are as filthy as death.

Our Lord says we can bear fruit only if we abide in Him and He in us, because apart from Him we can do nothing. This does not mean that we cannot do anything at all, but that even if we can do many things, they do not count before God. Whatever we can do by ourselves without needing to fellowship with God or to contact Him in spirit is neither of the spirit nor of life and is incapable of ministering life. Hence, it has no value and does not count before God. Not only so, it is even condemned by God. Therefore, we must learn to come out of this kind of work and turn within to contact God in spirit. Unless we do this, we would rather not do any work. We must force ourselves to such an extent that we absolutely must contact God in spirit. Otherwise, regardless of how much we can do, our work will still be condemned by God and will not be acceptable to Him.

THE DISCIPLINE OF GOD

For this reason, God often disciplines us through outward circumstances. He arranges persons, matters, or things to deal with our being, including our mind, emotion, and will. For example, you may be a person who is very thoughtful and who always likes to use the mind. Your mind always comes first in your dealing with any matter. Unless God deals with you severely, it will be difficult for someone like you to realize how terrible your mind is. If you do not allow God to enlighten you to such an extent so that you see that your thoughts must be condemned before Him, then it will not be easy for you to put them aside. Therefore, God raises up certain environments to do a breaking work on you. When you look back on some of the things that happened to you, you will become clear that they were solely to deal with your mind with its thoughts. You are a person with a thoughtful mind, so God allows you to encounter some situations which are beyond your comprehension. God especially uses these situations to deal with your thinking, your intelligence, your cleverness. People like you who are so clever and have much intelligence and who like to use their minds must be dealt with by God if they do not allow Him to enlighten them. If God is not successful in trying to enlighten you by His light, then He must strike you with the environment to deal especially with the clever mind which you always love to use.

A person might be very clever formerly, but after he has been dealt with by God, even though we cannot say he is no longer clever, his cleverness has been broken. Such a person cannot use his cleverness any longer. When you touch him, you can still tell that he was born a very clever person, but you feel that his cleverness has been broken by God. When he faces any situation now, he does not dare use his cleverness; rather, he is afraid of it. This is not to say that he is no longer clever, but he is afraid to use his cleverness. He has been struck and dealt with by God. He has suffered in his cleverness. His cleverness is still here, but it has been broken. In this breaking there is the release of the spirit. When he encounters any situation now, he uses his spirit to feel. Instead of using his mind, he uses his spirit first, and instead of acting according to his thinking, he acts according to the sense of his spirit.

With someone who is rich in emotion and who lives in his emotion, God will also raise up environments to strike and touch his emotion. In this kind of dealing, God's hand usually strikes precisely and heavily. After a person has been struck by God in his emotion, whenever he touches the Lord's work or meets with certain situations again, he will be afraid of his emotion and will not dare use it. This does not mean that he becomes a wooden person. Rather, it means that his emotion has been dealt with and broken by God and can no longer occupy the first place within him. Once the emotion is broken, the spirit within can come out and have a chance. This is God's purpose in raising up environments to discipline us.

Someone may have a very strong will and live entirely according to his will. With such a person, his will becomes his spiritual problem. His will hinders him from living in spirit and disables him from serving God in spirit. He may have some sense regarding this problem and may even have been enlightened by God, but he is not willing to learn to reject his will in every situation. Therefore, God arranges and raises up some circumstances to deal with him until his will has been broken and subdued. When you touch him after this, on the one hand, you can sense that he has a strong will, but on the other hand, you can also feel that his human will has been struck and broken. You can see that his spirit is released and strong. Whenever he touches the service of God, it is his spirit instead of his will that comes first.

The sufferings we face and the circumstances we encounter are mostly to deal with our natural man and the things in our soul. Many times our mind, emotion, and will all require God's environmental dealings. These things are not easily broken without the dealings in our environment. If these things are not broken, then the spirit within, the life within, which is our inner man, cannot be released. In order to release our spirit from within, God often uses the environment to break our outer man, our outer shell.

GOD'S TEARING DOWN

This is shown in 2 Corinthians 4, which says, "We have this treasure in earthen vessels" (v. 7). We know that *this treasure* denotes the Lord's life. The Lord's life is truly a treasure that we have obtained. However, since this treasure is put into an earthen vessel, it is not easily manifested, so God must come in to break the earthen vessel. The earthen vessel refers to our outer man. God uses the environment to deal with our outer man, that is, to break the earthen vessel. Through the environmental dealing and breaking, God puts to death our outer man. The afflictions we have due to God's dealing and breaking are just like death working in us to break us as earthen vessels. This is to break our outer man, which is our soul and all the things of our soul. After our outer man passes through the breaking of death, the Lord's life, which is the treasure in us, and our inner man, which is our spirit indwelt by the Lord's life, are released. Although the outer man is decaying, the inner man, the regenerated spirit, is being renewed and is growing stronger day by day. The outer man is broken, but the treasure in the inner man is released.

Regardless of how good the things released from our outer man—our soul—are, they are not the treasure within us. Rather, they frustrate that treasure from being released. For this reason, while we are pursuing the growth in life, God often raises certain circumstances to do a work of breaking, consuming, and tearing down in us. If you are a thoughtful person, God will raise up circumstances to deal particularly with your mind in order to break it and tear it down. If you are one who is rich in emotion or one who loves to use your will, God will arrange environments to deal specifically with your emotion or will in order to break them and tear them down. Whichever part of your soul is especially prominent, that is the part that God will come in to deal with specifically, and you will experience particular sufferings in that part. This may be compared to our face hitting a wall; the part of our face that hits first and suffers most is our nose, the most protruding part of our face. Whatever part is especially prominent or strong will be especially touched by God when we meet with His dealing, and that is the part that will truly feel the pain. If your will is especially strong, then it will be the first part touched by God's dealing, and it will be the part in which you feel the most pain. If your emotion is especially rich or your mind exceptionally sharp, then they will be the first parts touched by the circumstances given by God. You will suffer particularly in the point in which you are strong. Wherever you suffer the most is the place where you most need to be broken, because that is the point that has become a hindrance and an enemy to your spirit. If that particular point is not broken or torn down, then there will be no possibility for your spirit, your inner man, and the Lord's life within it to be released. This is why God must come in to break and tear down that particular point.

After we are saved or revived, in our pursuit of the spiritual growth, God comes to us not to build up but to tear down what we originally had. He will tear down our mind with its cleverness, our emotion with its zeal, and our will with its opinions. Oh, brothers and sisters, God's salvation is not to build up the things of the self in us. No, God's salvation is to build up His own things in us, to build up the things of Christ, the spiritual things, so that the spirit of life in us, that is, our new inner man, can grow stronger day by day, and the things we had originally, that is, everything of our old man, can be torn down and broken.

SPIRITUAL DISCERNMENT

If we see this point, we will clearly know where our service should be: not in the outer man but in the inner man; not in the soul but in the spirit; not in the mind, emotion, or will but in the spirit of life. If we know this and have this experience, we will be able to discern if a person's service is from the spirit or from the soul. We will not try to determine someone's worth before God according to what he is and does outwardly. We will be able to touch a person's inner parts to know if his living today is in the soul or in the spirit and to know if he is living in the soul or in the spirit.

A great deal of man's praises today are immature and inaccurate. For example, a certain brother may have some good points or strong points which are all of the self. Many brothers and sisters, however, praise him as being very spiritual. His living and what he is and does have not touched the spirit but are all in the soul and the self. Therefore, the brothers and sisters who praise him as being spiritual are inexperienced. Simply because he has strengths and good points does not mean that he is spiritual. Just because he does the right thing does not mean that he has acted spiritually. We still must ask and touch whether his strengths, good points, and being right are from the spirit or from the soul. Has his soul truly been broken by God? Has God dealt with his mind, emotion, and will? Has God torn down the self in him? Has he ever met God? Has he ever been touched by God? If you have had these kinds of experiences, then when you touch others, you will be able to tell if they are living in the soul or in the spirit. You will be able to sense that this brother, although he is good and right, is living actually in the soul and has never been broken. He is altogether a natural man. All of his living may be well-disciplined and perfect, but it is from the self and not from God. You can discern this; you have such a discerning ability.

THE MIND, EMOTION, AND WILL
OF A SPIRITUAL MAN

Some may ask, If our mind, emotion, and will are all broken, will we not become simpletons? No, God breaks our mind, emotion, and will, but does not nullify them. We still have them. Furthermore, the mind of a truly spiritual person is many times sharper than it was before, his will is many times stronger, and his emotion is many times richer. The more spiritual a person is, the sharper his mind, the richer his emotion, and the stronger his will. The spiritual man, however, does not allow these things to take the preeminence. Rather, his spirit takes the first place. Whenever he encounters a situation, he lets his spirit come in first, and only then does he use his mind, emotion, and will. When he rejects his mind, emotion, and will and allows his spirit to come first in this way, the result is that his mind becomes sharper, his emotion richer, and his will stronger. The Spirit of God has the ground within him and rules not only in his spirit but also in his mind, so his mind becomes sharper and wiser. This is the natural outcome. The more a person denies himself, the wiser his mind will be. If a person only wants the Lord and rejects himself, he will be the wisest person because the Spirit of God is in him, and no one can be wiser than the Spirit of God. In this universe, is there anyone wiser than the Spirit of God? Since the Spirit of God reigns in him and enters into his inward parts to such an extent, it is no wonder that he is wise! He has the Holy Spirit not only in his spirit, but he has the Holy Spirit even in his mind. Because the Holy Spirit has gained the ground in him to enter his mind, his mind becomes very wise.

It is the same with the emotion. The most spiritual person must be the one with the richest emotion. The emotionless ones are the non-spiritual ones. Suppose a person sees something good but cannot appreciate it, encounters a sad situation but cannot cry, meets with a happy event but cannot laugh, or does not know what difficulty and ease are, because to him suffering and joy, difficulty and ease, make no difference. In this case, he has no way to be spiritual. Every spiritual person is rich in emotion because the God who has entered him and filled his emotion is rich in emotion. Because such ones allow God to reign in them, His Spirit can enter into their emotion. Therefore, they are definitely abounding in emotions. Many times they shed more tears than others, and they also laugh more joyfully than others. Like the spiritual apostle Paul, they are truly joyful when they are happy and truly sorrowful when they are sad. Although they are richer than others in emotion, they are not wild but restrained. They are directed and governed inwardly by the Holy Spirit. When you touch their emotion, you sense that they are full of the presence of God within them. Although they are rich in emotion, they do not live in their emotion; instead, they live in their spirit.

In the same way, a spiritual person also has a very strong will. This is because the Holy Spirit reigns in him to strengthen his will. The more spiritual a person is, the stronger his will. At the same time, the more spiritual a person is, the more pliable his will. The will of a spiritual person is strong, on the one hand, and pliable, on the other hand. It can stand up and it can also bend. It is truly both strong and pliant. Such a person submits to God's authority, allowing the Spirit of God to enter and rule over his will so that his will is balanced between strength and pliancy. When he should be firm, he is firm; when he should bend, he bends.

Thus, it does not mean that if one lives in and by his spirit, then he loses his mind, emotion, and will. On the contrary, the more a person lives in and by his spirit, the sharper his mind is, the richer his emotion is, and the stronger his will is, because the Holy Spirit dominates him and reigns in him. The Holy Spirit within him has the ground and is able to enter and reign in every part of his being, including his mind, emotion, and will. Thus, every part of his being, under the strengthening and control of the Holy Spirit, not only becomes stronger but also is used properly.

Therefore, we must see that once we live in the spirit and allow it to have the proper ground in us, the mind, emotion, and will of our soul will be strengthened and made normal. We must remember, however, that they are of secondary importance and that the spirit is of primary importance. They are under the direction of the spirit as the source, the preeminent part, and the dominant part. In every matter we should begin from the spirit, allowing the spirit to come in first. Then we should allow the spirit to direct and control every part of our being. If we do this, and only then, our living and service will be of the spirit, in the spirit, touching the spirit, and supplying others with the spirit. May God bless us in this way!

CHAPTER EIGHT

THE SERVICE WHICH IS FROM GOD

Scripture Reading: 2 Cor. 3:5-6

Not that we are sufficient of ourselves to account anything as from ourselves; but our sufficiency is from God, who has also made us sufficient as ministers of a new covenant, ministers not of the letter but of the Spirit; for the letter kills, but the Spirit gives life.

TWO SOURCES OF SERVICE

Each of the two Bible verses above mentions two different sources. The two mentioned in verse 5 are "ourselves" and "God," and the two in verse 6 are "letter" and "Spirit." Although these two verses speak of four sources, it does not mean that our service has four different sources. These four sources are actually only two. The first two sources are embodied in and joined with the latter two. Just as "ourselves" is joined with "letter," so "God" is also one with "Spirit." Just as serving God by the letter is actually serving God by ourselves, so also serving God by the Spirit is serving God by God Himself. If we intend to serve God by ourselves, we must serve by the letter. Likewise, if we intend to serve God by God Himself, we must serve by the Spirit. Just as the service by the letter is the service in ourselves and from ourselves, so also the service by the Spirit is the service in God and from God. Therefore, there are only two kinds of services with two kinds of sources. One kind of service is by the letter and from ourselves, and the other kind is by the Spirit and from God. If our service is not from the first source, then it is from the second source, and if it is not from ourselves, then it is from God. Or conversely, if it is not from God, then it is from ourselves. Besides these, there is no third source.

THE SERVICE WHICH IS FROM GOD

We do not have time to closely examine these two sources of our service. We can only consider one of these two: the service which is from God. This kind of service is not from ourselves or by ourselves, and of course, it is also not for ourselves. Rather, it is from God and by God, and certainly it is also for God. The service which is from ourselves takes ourselves as its source, and it is performed by us according to the ordinances and rituals of the letter. It can be carried out by us outside of God and independently of God, without any need to rely on God, seek God, or fellowship with God. But the service which is from God is not like this! It requires us to rely on God, seek God, fellowship with God, be in God, and absolutely take God as our source. This kind of service is not from man's wisdom, does not rely on man's power, and is not for man's pleasure. Rather, it is from God's revelation, relies on the Holy Spirit of God, and is for God's purpose. Hence, it requires us to live in and by the spirit. We must reject the mind, emotion, and will of the soul and live in the spirit and by the sense of the spirit, walking according to the leading of the spirit. Only then can we have fellowship with God and receive His revelation to render the service which is from God, which takes God as its source, which relies on God, and which is for God.

THE NECESSITY
OF FELLOWSHIPPING WITH GOD

This kind of service from God requires us to have fellowship with God and not be detached from God. In order to have this kind of service, we must be in fellowship with God; we cannot act independently of God, God and we being separated. Every service that is from God and pleasing to Him is carried out by contacting and touching Him. We serve Him while contacting Him. We cannot stand apart from Him and lose touch with Him. If we serve outside of Him, regardless of whether by our zeal or anything else, our service is not from Him and therefore has no spiritual value. A service which is from God and has spiritual value must be one in which we are joined to God and in fellowship with Him by abiding in Him. On the one hand, He operates within us, and on the other hand, we serve Him outwardly. Therefore, this kind of service is an activity issuing out of God's operation within us. Outwardly, we are serving Him, yet inwardly He is operating.

Brother Andrew Murray said that prayer is the Christ within us praying to the Christ on the throne. This word is both deep and to the point. What is prayer? Prayer is Christ praying to Christ, and it merely passes through us. A genuine, spiritual prayer does not originate with us or come from us and is not prayed by ourselves alone. Rather, it originates with Christ and comes from Christ and is prayed by the Christ abiding in us to the Christ sitting on the throne.

Just as it is with prayer, so it is also with all other kinds of service. Any kind of service must be a service rendered through us by the God abiding in us to the God sitting on the throne. This is the service which God wants and accepts. We cannot serve Him without Him having any ground in us. We cannot merely serve Him on earth and He merely receives it in heaven—He and we, we and He, standing apart from each other instead of being joined with one another. We cannot merely think of Him one minute and then immediately serve Him zealously without contacting Him or being mingled with Him. This kind of service is from ourselves and by ourselves, not from God or by God. Therefore, it has no element of God in it.

The apostle said that his service in the new covenant was not from himself or by himself; it was from God and by God. It is true that he served God, but it was more a matter of God operating in him and bringing him along to serve God. He served God not because he was happy and convinced and therefore made up his mind to do something for God. No! He served God because he gave and yielded himself to the indwelling God, putting his mind, emotion, and will under God's control to be occupied and filled by God. In this way God was able to gain all the ground in him and to operate in him through His Spirit, motivating him to work and serve. Because he was moved by God inwardly, there was a strength that compelled him to serve outwardly. He was not compelled by his own zeal or his mind, emotion, and will. No! It was God in him, mingling with him and motivating him to serve. This service did not come out of himself; instead, it came out of God. Apparently, it was he serving; actually, it was God operating and motivating within him.

Before Paul was saved, he was Saul. At that time he also served God, but his service then was not from God but from himself. He was exceedingly zealous for God according to the religious education he had received. He was a young man with a strong will and great passion, with talents and courage. He served God with these qualities according to the Jewish religious ordinances. In such a service there was no ground for God or the element of God. Such a service was not from God or by God but from himself and by himself. At that time he served God by his own zeal, courage, and talent instead of by God.

After he was saved, God lived in him and he was joined to God. He and God were no longer two, but the two became one. God's life became his life, God's nature became his nature, God's feeling became his feeling, and God's view became his view. God's everything became his everything, his content. When he gave God the ground in him in this way, and when he and God fellowshipped together, God operated in him, giving him a sense that motivated him to serve God by preaching the gospel. His service was from God and by God. It issued from his passing through God and allowing God to pass through him. This kind of service was not just a work or an enterprise but the flowing out of God and the overflow of God's life.

In the matter of service we cannot do it out of our enthusiasm, determination, or capability, nor can we serve merely according to what we were taught. None of these things should be the source of our service. The source of our service should be God, it should be the spirit, it should be God's operation in us, and it should be the operation, direction, and leading of the Spirit of God in our spirit. Only the service which comes out of these things is the service which is from God and by God.

Therefore, it is not possible to have the service which is from God without meeting, touching, or contacting Him. We must meet Him, touch Him, and contact Him inwardly in order to be able to render the service which is from Him. For example, some preach the gospel merely out of their zeal and excitement without touching, meeting, or fellowshipping with God. Their preaching of the gospel in this way is from themselves; it is not motivated by God's operation in them. In contrast, others preach the gospel because, while they were drawing near to God, confessing their sins before Him, and dealing with all the things that are not pleasing to Him, they have received the burden from the Spirit of the Lord who has gained the ground to operate and motivate in them. Their preaching of the gospel in this way is not motivated by their zeal. Rather, it is the Holy Spirit motivating them inwardly like a burning fire, causing them to be desperate to preach the gospel to their friends and relatives. This situation is like an electric fan; after coming into contact with electricity, the fan begins to turn by the inward driving force of the electricity. This kind of gospel preaching is from God and is spiritual. This is to serve God, and this is to serve God by Him and through Him. This kind of service cannot be disconnected or separated from God.

When we render service to God, we cannot be detached from Him. Rather, we must rely on Him moment by moment. Therefore, it is not sufficient merely to have experience and thus know how to do things and know how to serve God. Serving God can never depend on our "know how." You cannot say that because you were able to give a good message yesterday, so today you can give the same message again. Yesterday you spoke by relying on God; today when you speak, you still must rely on God. Service to God is carried out not by relying on experience but by depending on God through fellowship and contact with Him.

Some have often said to me, "Brother Lee, teach us some of the secrets of service, because once we have the secrets, we will be able to do it." I said, "There is not such a thing! If there were any secrets to serving God, it would be this one secret: fellowship with God." One can do anything for a long period of time and be considered a veteran, an experienced hand, in that thing. However, this is not possible in the service of God. Serving God requires a moment-by-moment, fresh contact with God. The electric fan cannot say that because it has been turning for two years, it has become a "veteran," an "experienced hand," and does not need to contact the electricity anymore. Regardless of how long it has been turning, it must maintain its contact with electricity. On the first day it turns, it must contact the electricity, and on the last day it turns, it still must contact the electricity. Even if we have served God for a long time, we still need to contact Him. Even Paul would have to contact God if he were here serving today. He could not say that he is an old-timer, so he does not need to contact God or fellowship with Him. If this were the case, what he would do would be merely a work, and God's element could not be found in his work.

Our service and our work are not so much a matter of having some accomplishments as they are a matter of expressing God and flowing out His life. If we do not serve or work according to God, and if we do not have the presence of God, then how can He be expressed or flowed out in what we do? Therefore, our service must come from our fellowship with God and our relying on Him. Every time we serve, we must fellowship with God and allow Him to operate in us. We must set aside our excitement, thoughts, and opinions to allow Him to gain the ground in us, to fill us, and to operate in us. This is the source of our service, and it is the most precious source.

In the early days, in the church in Antioch there were five prophets and teachers. While they were praying together, ministering to the Lord, and fellowshipping with Him, the Holy Spirit came and sent two of them out to work for the Lord. These five men did not hold a meeting for discussion or use their mind to think and then make a decision to send two of them out to work. It was not like that at all! They gave themselves to the Lord and allowed Him to have the ground in them. Under these circumstances, the Lord was able to get through and operate in them, thus sending them out to preach the gospel. When they went out, they were filled with

God, relying on Him, and brought Him with them. When people came across this kind of work, what they felt and obtained was not a thing, but God and the life of God.

Is our work for the accomplishing of an enterprise or is it for the overflowing and release of God? If we want our work to flow out and release God, then we must learn to reject our zeal, thought, emotion, and decisions and to always prostrate ourselves before God, looking to Him and fellowshipping with Him. We should do this not only when we pray, but all the time we should be fellowshipping with God inwardly, giving Him the throne and authority in us, allowing Him to occupy us and operate in us as He pleases. When we fellowship with God in this way and allow Him to occupy us, He can easily reveal His heart's desire to us and flow Himself out of us. This is especially true of the brothers who are elders in the churches. If they do not receive God's leading in fellowship, God's burden, or God's commission, then the service in the local churches will rarely flow out God.

Some brothers who are elders have asked me how they can receive a burden or commission from God. The way is this: You should turn yourself to God, allow Him to occupy your every part, and give Him the first place in every part. Instead of allowing your emotion, mind, and will to be number one, you should give Him the preeminence in you. Thus, when you draw near to God and fellowship with Him, it will be easy for you to receive God's burden. God gives His burden only to this kind of people. If you give God the ground and opportunity, then it will be easy for God to operate in you, causing you to receive a commission and a burden. This kind of burden causes your service to be a service that comes out of God's motivation within you. Hence, you will be able to flow out and release God.

THE NECESSITY
OF BEING ABLE TO MINISTER LIFE

Thus, the service which is from God requires us to have fellowship with God and minister life to others. The service which God wants from us does not focus on doing a work but on ministering life. The center and goal of the service of the saints and of the church are not to build up an enterprise or a work but to minister God's life. It does not matter what profession the worldly people are in—farming, business, industry, education; all emphasize having a successful enterprise. If their enterprise is successful, then they have reached their goal. However, the service of the church and of the saints is not like this! The service of the church and of the saints is nothing and worthless in God's eyes if all we have done is successfully finish our work, having built up either a big or a small enterprise. God's desire is that the emphasis of our service be on ministering God's life instead of producing a work or enterprise.

For the sake of the new believers, we will use words that are easily understood to explain this. For example, the church is here serving God, but the emphasis is not on how many meeting halls are built, how many enterprises are established, how many activities are carried out, how much work is done, or how many people are brought in. These are not the center and goal of the church service. To use these items to measure and judge the church service is a huge mistake. How weighty the church service is, how high it is, how much value it has, and how acceptable it is in God's eyes—all these are not measured by the aforementioned items as the standard, such as the number of people, the material things, the size of the enterprise, and the amount of work. Rather, the only standard of measurement is how much the church has ministered God's life to others and how much element of the divine life has entered into people through the church's help and service.

God measures the work and service of the church according to one point: how much supply of spiritual life the church has given people and how much increase of the element of God's life people have received when they were helped by the church. God uses only this standard to measure the church's service. Even if we were to bring all the people in this locality into the church, convert all the houses into meeting halls, and stir up so many people to zealously preach the gospel, in God's eyes it would all be empty and worthless unless these people have the divine life, are filled with some of the divine element, have received enough of God, and have sufficient knowledge of God. God absolutely does not measure our service and work by anything apart from Himself. He measures our service and work only by how much of His element people have gained and been filled with inwardly. It is not that our service and our work are weighty before God if we build huge meeting halls, do things in an orderly way, or have large numbers of people. There is not such a thing! The weight of our service and work does not depend on the number of people, things, and activities. Instead, it depends on the amount of God's life people have touched, gained, been filled with, and experienced. It is not that our service, our work, is weighty if we gain a few more people, do a few more activities, and obtain a few more things. We can never use these as the standard for measuring our service and work. We must see how much our service and work have ministered the divine life to others. Some do not have the divine life yet, but after our contact with them and our help to them, God's life gets into them. Others have a little of God's life but are very immature and have only a shallow knowledge of God, but after our contact and fellowship with them, they have a deeper desire for God inwardly, they pursue God more deeply, and they gain more of His life.

Our service and work should only minister God's life to people and should only use God's life to attract people. When people come to our meetings, we should give them the sense that they have touched the spirit, met God, and received the supply of life. We should not let them feel that they have touched some other good things besides these items. Perhaps our meeting halls are primitive with only a small number in the meetings, but once a person enters our meetings, he senses the presence of God and touches God. When a person walks into this kind of meeting, he has an indescribable sensation that his darkness has turned into light, that he has found a way through his difficulties, that his weaknesses have been made strong, and that he has been uplifted from his depression.

The corporate service of the church should be like this, as should our individual service. When people contact us, even just for a moment, they should gain the help of life inwardly. It is as if we have something which comes out from within us and touches them inwardly to enliven them. They were in darkness inwardly, but after contacting us for a moment, they are enlightened. In the past they were lacking in their inward knowledge of the life of God, but after contacting us for a moment their knowledge improves and increases. We bring them into the Lord and enable them to receive the supply of life. The help which they receive from us is not material, social, emotional, or doctrinal. Rather, it is spiritual, of life, from God, and in Christ. What they obtain from us in life in this way is truly God Himself and the divine life.

In our work we should not use other things to attract people. We should not use social contacts, money, or anything apart from God because all these things belong to death. In our work we should only attract people with God and minister His life to them. Only this kind of service is spiritual, is from God, and is able to touch God.

In John 15 the Lord says that He is the vine and we are the branches. Apart from the vine, the branches can do nothing. The branches on the vine are not there to be its material; they are there to bear fruit. Bearing fruit is to minister life, that is, to release the supply of the vine's life. This is our function with respect to the Lord. Today the Lord does not need people to be His material, nor does He need human talent. He only needs people to abide in Him, to be filled with Him, and to release the supply of His life. This is truly like the branches of the vine being filled with the sap of the vine and releasing the supply of the vine's life. The branches of the vine do not know how to do anything but abide in the vine and allow its life to be ministered and to flow out through them.

This is the service of the church, which is not a great work or large enterprise with a huge accomplishment but the ministering and flowing out of the life of Christ. It requires us to be joined to Christ, to abide in Christ, and to give Him the ground in us to fill us, so that His life, His nature, His likes, and His inclination can become our life, our nature, our likes, and our inclination. In other words, His all becomes our all. When we abide in Him, live in Him, and fellowship with Him like this, we allow Him to pass through us and flow out from us. What flows out from us is His life, the life of the vine. This will minister life to others, and it will give them life. When people touch this, they touch Christ and the life of the vine. This is the service of the church.

George Müller, who founded an orphanage in England, was such a person living in God to serve God. Unfortunately, however, some of the biographies written about him place too much emphasis on the success of his enterprise while neglecting the matters of his spiritual life, such as his abiding in God and living before Him. When I read his journal, I did not feel that he was operating a large business. I only felt that I was touching a person who lived before God, fellowshipped with God, allowed God to rule in him, allowed God to have a place in him, and was filled with God inwardly. Every time I read his journal, I was brought before God and given the sense of God's presence. This made me feel that Müller was one who lived in the light and who lived before God. You touch God when you read his writings. This is the life of George Müller; it is not a life that emphasized a successful enterprise but a life that knew God and flowed out His divine life.

We must always remember that the service of the church is God's flowing out to supply others with the divine life. It is not a matter of how many things we accomplish or how many works we do. Instead, it is a matter of how much God we flow out and how much of God's life we minister to others. This is where all the issues lie! God never uses other things to judge our work. He only uses His life to judge our work. The more our work has God Himself and the element of His life, the weightier and more valuable it is. If we do not have this, then our work is empty and a failure.

May God truly have mercy on us that all our service and work would be from Him, would come out of our fellowship with Him, and would be able to overflow with Him and His life as a supply to others.

ABOUT THE AUTHOR

Witness Lee was born in 1905 in northern China and raised in a Christian family. At age 19 he was fully captured for Christ and immediately consecrated himself to preach the gospel for the rest of his life. Early in his service, he met Watchman Nee, a renowned preacher, teacher, and writer. Witness Lee labored together with Watchman Nee under his direction. In 1934 Watchman Nee entrusted Witness Lee with the responsibility for his publication operation, called the Shanghai Gospel Bookroom.

Prior to the Communist takeover in 1949, Witness Lee was sent by Watchman Nee and his other co-workers to Taiwan to insure that the things delivered to them by the Lord would not be lost. Watchman Nee instructed Witness Lee to continue the former's publishing operation abroad as the Taiwan Gospel Bookroom, which has been publicly recognized as the publisher of Watchman Nee's works outside China. Witness Lee's work in Taiwan manifested the Lord's abundant blessing. From a mere 350 believers, newly fled from the mainland, the churches in Taiwan grew to 20,000 in five years.

In 1962 Witness Lee felt led of the Lord to come to the United States, settling in California. During his 35 years of service in the U.S., he ministered in weekly meetings and weekend conferences, delivering several thousand spoken messages. Much of his speaking has since been published as over 400 titles. Many of these have been translated into over fourteen languages. He gave his last public conference in February 1997 at the age of 91.

He leaves behind a prolific presentation of the truth in the Bible. His major work, *Life-study of the Bible,* comprises over 25,000 pages of commentary on every book of the Bible from the perspective of the believers' enjoyment and experience of God's divine life in Christ through the Holy Spirit. Witness Lee was the chief editor of a new translation of the New Testament into Chinese called the Recovery Version and directed the translation of the same into English. The Recovery Version also appears in a number of other languages. He provided an extensive body of footnotes, outlines, and spiritual cross references. A radio broadcast of his messages can be heard on Christian radio stations in the United States. In 1965 Witness Lee founded Living Stream Ministry, a non-profit corporation, located in Anaheim, California, which officially presents his and Watchman Nee's ministry.

Witness Lee's ministry emphasizes the experience of Christ as life and the practical oneness of the believers as the Body of Christ. Stressing the importance of attending to both these matters, he led the churches under his care to grow in Christian life and function. He was unbending in his conviction that God's goal is not narrow sectarianism but the Body of Christ. In time, believers began to meet simply as the church in their localities in response to this conviction. In recent years a number of new churches have been raised up in Russia and in many eastern European countries.